TEEN MINDFULNESS SKILLS WORKBOOK:
Remedies for Worry, Anxiety & Stress

A Practitioner's Guide to Teaching Mindfulness Skills

Ester R.A. Leutenberg • John J. Liptak, EdD
with Niki Tilicki, MA Ed

publisher of therapy, counseling, and self-help resources

101 West 2nd Street, Suite 203
Duluth, MN 55802

800-247-6789

Books@WholePerson.com
WholePerson.com

Teen Mindfulness Skills Workbook: Remedies for Worry, Anxiety & Stress

Copyright ©2019 by Ester R.A. Leutenberg, John J. Liptak, EdD with Niki Tilicki, MA Ed. All rights reserved. The activities, assessment tools, and handouts in this workbook are reproducible by the purchaser for educational or therapeutic purposes. No other part of this workbook may be reproduced or transmitted in any form by any means, electronic, or mechanical without permission in writing from the publisher.

All efforts have been made to ensure the accuracy of the information contained in this workbook as of the date published.
The author(s) and the publisher expressly disclaim responsibility for any adverse effects arising from the use or application of the information contained herein.

Editorial Directors: Jack Kosmach and Carlene Sippola
Art Director: Mathew Pawlak
Cover Design: Adam Sippola

Library of Congress Control Number: 2018963203
ISBN: 978-1-57025-356-0

Our gratitude to all of these professionals who make us look good:

Art Director – Mathew Pawlak
Editor – Eileen Regen, M Ed, CJE
Copy Editor – Peg Johnson
Editorial Directors – Jack Kosmach and Carlene Sippola
Proof-reader – Jay Leutenberg

Carol Butler Cooper, MS Ed, RN, C
Annette Damien, MS, PPS
Beth Jennings, M Ed
Xanthe Philips
Peggy Shecket, MS
Niki Tilicki, MA Ed

Thank You!
Ester Leutenberg and John Liptak

Using this Workbook

This workbook has been designed as a practical tool for counselors, social workers, teachers, group leaders, therapists, and other helping professionals. Depending on the role of the professional using *Teen Mindfulness Skills Workbook: Remedies for Worry, Anxiety & Stress,* the modules can be used either individually or as part of an integrated mindfulness curriculum. The facilitator may choose to use this program with clients who need to slow down, live more in the present moment, pay attention rather than live on autopilot, and accept life and others without being judgmental. The activities in this workbook can be used with individual clients or with groups. The techniques used in the assessment tool and self-exploration activities are evidence-based and field-tested.

Format of the Workbook

The *Teen Mindfulness Skills Workbook: Remedies for Worry, Anxiety & Stress* contains a mindfulness assessment and many guided self-exploration activities in the chapters that can be used to enhance mindfulness and create greater well-being. The assessment can be used as a pre-test to discover participants' mindful state before training, and then used again as a post-test at the end of training to see the effects of the training. The purpose of this assessment (and any quick assessments throughout the chapters) is not to categorize people, but to allow them to explore various elements that are critical for success in developing mindfulness. This workbook contains self-assessments and not tests. Traditional tests measure knowledge and elicit either right or wrong responses. These assessments ask only for opinions or attitudes about topics related to a variety of coping skills and abilities.

In addition to the assessments, each chapter includes a set of guided self-exploration activities to help participants learn how to develop mindfulness in their daily lives. The activities assist participants in self-reflection and the practice of mindfulness techniques. These brief, easy-to-use self-reflection tools are designed to promote insight and self-growth. Many different types of guided self-exploration activities are provided, so you may pick and choose the activities most suited and appealing to your participants. Many of the guided self-exploration activities include a journaling component that allows participants to gain insights into themselves and more effective ways of living their lives. The guided self-exploration activities are reproducible; you may photocopy as many pages as you wish for your participants.

Free PDF Download Available

To access your free PDF download of the assessment tools and all of the reproducible activities in this workbook, go to WholePerson.com/store/MindfulnessSkillsTeens3203.html.

Table of Contents

Introduction viii
Chapter Descriptions xi
Mindfulness Assessment xiii

CHAPTER 1

Are You on Autopilot? 17
   What are Your Daily Hassles? 22
   What are Your Difficult Hassles? 23
   How Mindful are You? 24
   Are You Living on Autopilot? 25
   What's Wearing You Down? 26
   Are Your Old Habits Positive or Negative? 27
   How is Worry, Anxiety & Stress
      Effecting You? 28
   Can You Slow Down? 29
   When Do You Zone Out? 30
   Do you Celebrate the Little Things? 31
   What are Two Daily Worries, Anxieties,
      and/or Stressors? 32
   How Do You Start the Day? 33
   Do You Have a Restless Mind? 34
   Are You Comfortable Being with Yourself? 35
   How Can You Become More Aware? 36
   Quotes about Autopilot 37

CHAPTER 2

Do You Pay Full Attention? 39
   Does Your Mind Wander? 44
   Can You Control Your Focus? 45
   Do You Get Caught Up in
      Negative Feelings? 46
   Are You Always Aware of Your Actions? . . . 47
   Do You Bring Purpose to What You Do? . . . 48
   Are You Aware of Being Mindful? 49
   How Do You React to Worry,
      Anxiety & Stress? 50
   What is Your Habitual Reaction? 51
   Do You Engage in "What If..." Thinking? . . 52
   How is Your Attention Span? 53
   What are Your INTERNAL Forces? 54
   What are Your EXTERNAL Forces? 55
   Are You Aware of Your Mental State? 56
   Can You Change the Moment? 57
   Do You Take the Time to Smell the Roses? 58
   Quotes about Paying Attention 59

CHAPTER 3

Can You Stay in the Present Moment? . . 61
   Do You Tend to Focus on
      the Present or the Past? 66
   How is Your Breath a Gift? 67
   Do You Learn Your Lesson? 68
   Do You Go With the Flow? 69
   Do You Get Caught Up in the Future? 70
   Are Your Routines
      Becoming TOO Routine? 71
   How "Should" You Be? 72
   Do You Multi-Task or Uni-Task? 73
   Can You Slow Down, You Crazy Child? . . . 74
   Do You Think Too Much? 75
   Are You Present When Listening? 76
   Quotes about Being Present 77

(Continued on the next page)

Table of Contents

CHAPTER 4

**Do You Accept Others Using
  Wise Judgment?** 79

Do You Judge Others Wisely? 84

Are You Aware of
  Your Judgmental Thoughts? 85

How Accepting of Other People Are You? .. 86

Do You Accept Situations
  for What They Are? 87

Do You Sometimes Judge Too Fast? 88

What is an Opinionated,
  Judgmental Person? 89

How Do You Judge Yourself? 90

How Do You Negatively Judge Others? ... 91

Are You Objective? 92

How Do You Show Empathy,
  Kindness, and Compassion? 93

How Do You Deal with Change? 94

Which Do You Do? 95

Do You Let Your Feelings Come and Go? .. 96

How Are You Being Threatened? 97

What Daily Hassles Fill You with
  Worry, Anxiety & Stress? 98

What is Happening When
  Someone is Mindful? 99

Quotes about
  Non-Judgmental Awareness 100

CHAPTER 5

**Do You Have a Backpack of
  Mindfulness Techniques?** 103

How Mindful Are You? 108

Do You Tune in to Your Sensations? 109

Can You Sense Your Senses? 111

How Can You Start Your Day Mindfully? 112

How Can You Reframe, then Detach,
  from Your Thoughts? 113

How Can You Activate Your Senses? ... 114

Can You Meditate While Walking? YES! .. 115

Can You Meditate While Concentrating
  on the Outdoors? YES! 116

What are Good Reasons to Meditate? ... 117

Where Can You Meditate? 118

How Can You Observe in a Mindful Way? 119

Have You Tried Mindful Meditation? ... 120

Can You Journal About Mindfulness? ... 121

Does Mindfulness Bring Awareness? ... 122

Do You Eat Mindfully? 123

Can You Bring Your Awareness
  to Your Breath? 124

What is Abdominal Breathing? 125

Have You Tried Breathing to
  Avoid Being Judgmental? 126

How Can You Practice
  Mindful Appreciation? 127

Can You Maintain Your Focus? 129

How Can You Be More Aware
  of Your Body? 130

Are You Thinking Again? 131

Can You Be Thankful? 132

Teen Mindfulness Skills Workbook: Remedies for Worry, Anxiety & Stress

Introduction

Wouldn't it be great if we were wired to automatically deal with everyday hassles in a calm, mindful way? That is not always the case. However, together with identifying the worry, anxiety, and stress of everyday hassles and practicing mindfulness exercises, we can learn to shift quickly into a "mindfulness mode" when a situation warrants it. We may even decide that some seemingly major issues are really everyday hassles that can be expected, experienced, and resolved using mindfulness tools. Throughout this workbook, we will explore the various aspects involved in developing mindfulness as the antidote to help in coping with these daily hassles and their effects.

Mindfulness is the process of developing your mind so that it is fully attending to what's currently happening, to what you are doing in the present moment, and to the space you are moving through. In most cases of daily hassles, random ideas begin to fly through your mind, you lose touch with your body and environment, and soon you are experiencing a variety of obsessive thoughts about something that just happened or fretting about the future. This process produces worry, anxiety, and stress.

What Is Mindfulness?

Mindfulness is about developing the basic human ability to be fully present, aware of where you are and what you are doing, and not overly reactive or overwhelmed by daily hassles. Mindfulness is a tremendous technique, one that is powerful for snapping you back to where you are in the present and what you are doing and feeling. While all people possess the ability to develop mindfulness, it is rarely activated and utilized when daily hassles build up and begin to cause stress and frustration. The good news is that mindfulness can be developed and cultivated through the techniques utilized in this workbook.

Mindfulness has been described as a state of mind in which people can observe mental activity without attaching to it or evaluating it. Mindfulness is about becoming aware of your natural tendency to sleepwalk through life. When on autopilot, you navigate through the day totally unaware of what you are doing. This happens when a driver arrives at work and does not even remember traveling there, or the person who is so busy thinking about the future that the beauty of the present is overlooked. Through mindfulness, people can recognize when they are operating on autopilot and step into the present moment free from worry, anxiety, and stress. It is paying attention on purpose, being present in your surroundings and with people, and enjoying and appreciating life more. Mindfulness is about paying attention to what is going on with the body, mind, and environment which leads to an understanding of how you are getting stuck in autopilot. By developing mindfulness, people can build a fresh perspective and start to become more aware of personal habits that cause stress, fear, dissatisfaction, frustration, and anger. With this awareness comes the ability to stop reacting to daily hassles and start to begin to make more effective life choices.

Why Is Mindfulness Important?

Although mindfulness is not automatic and does not occur spontaneously, it can be learned and practiced so that it can be accessed intentionally when it is needed. Some of the characteristics of mindfulness include non-judgmental awareness, paying attention on purpose, remaining non-judgmental, staying in the present, being non-reactive, and remaining openhearted and compassionate.

Mindfulness has many benefits that can help to reduce the stress associated with daily hassles:

- **Increased acceptance**—By not making evaluations, participants can accept the internal thoughts in their mind and see these messages as simple mental processes rather than pure truths.
- **Greater awareness**—Participants will be able to experience expanded awareness and a clearer vision of the world and its processes.
- **Less intense reactions**—Participants will be less inclined to react when experiencing the stress of daily hassles. Instead, they will develop an observer stance through which they are free from evaluation, attachment, and frustration.
- **Relaxed approach**—Participants will learn to cope with worry, anxiety, and stress related to daily hassles in life.
- **Calm demeanor**—Participants will develop a state of mind in which they are mentally and physically at peace. They will be prepared to deal more effectively with the daily worry, stress and hassles, and anxiety, and will then experience greater overall well-being.
- **Mental functioning**—Participants will experience greater concentration, focus, and self-awareness to promote greater personal and professional growth and development.

Don't We All Have Daily Hassles?

Throughout this workbook, teens will explore the ways that daily hassles can affect their levels of worry, anxiety, and stress; and thus, their overall well-being. Daily hassles can be described as the small, day to day irritations, repeated many times, that cause teens to worry, feel a heightened sense of anxiety, and feel stressed. Examples of daily hassles include frustrations such as occurrences when there are computer problems, losing keys, being stuck in traffic, not enough money for lunch, way too much homework, a sick parent who can't help with a project for school. Daily hassles are those irritating, frustrating, distressing demands that to some degree characterize our everyday transactions with the environment. The accumulation of minor daily hassles create persistent irritations, frustrations, and overloads which lead to more serious reactions such as chronic worry, anxiety, and stress. The following illustrates the process of moving from the irritation of daily hassles to a state of calm.

The Desired Process

Chapter Descriptions

The chapter titles and the activity page titles all ask questions to think about and respond to. They will help your client lead a more mindful life.

Chapter 1:
Are You on Autopilot?

This chapter will alert teens to wake-up calls, or reminders for them to not react immediately, but to come back to awareness so that they can be more mindful during daily activities. It will explore those stressors that wake us up to the calm that can be part of our everyday lives. When daily hassles affect participants, mindfulness triggers will remind them to break out of autopilot so they can be mindful, spontaneous, calm, and free.

Chapter 2:
Do You Pay Full Attention?

This chapter will focus on teens developing awareness of their own body, thoughts, and sensations that arise in their experience. It will provide activities to help in applying mindful awareness to all aspects of their bodily experience. Teens will be instructed to mindfully notice what they see, hear, taste, feel, and smell. They will be instructed on how to cultivate an open, curious, and gentle attitude of mindfulness towards what they sense and feel about the hassles occurring in their lives.

Chapter 3:
Can You Stay in the Present Moment?

This chapter will help teens choose to fully observe the events and feelings that are happening in their internal and external experiences right now. It will help participants let go of the need to continually focus on the past or the future and bring their full awareness to each moment in time.

Chapter 4:
Do You Accept Others By Using Wise Judgment?

This chapter will stress that in a state of true mindfulness, teens will choose to refrain from making any judgments about their daily hassle experiences, no matter how painful they may be. Mindfulness is not about solving problems and searching for solutions. Rather, it is more about observing your present-moment experiences with curiosity, openness, acceptance, and love. Teens will then be instructed to practice describing their internal and external experiences with non-judgmental language.

Chapter 5:
Do You Have a Backpack of Mindfulness Techniques?

This chapter will provide a variety of common mindfulness practices as well as unique practices that can be used in any situation or at any time to overcome worry, anxiety, and stress.

Mindfulness Assessment

The assessment on pages 5, 6, and 7 measures the main ideas in each of the four modules of this workbook.
- The first page (below) is the introduction and directions.
- The second page is the assessment.
- The third page includes the descriptions, scoring directions and profile interpretation.

This assessment can be used as a pre-test to assess participants' mindful state before training, and then used again as a post-test at the end of training to measure the effects of the mindfulness training.

Introduction and Directions

Mindfulness is a state of awareness in which people can observe events occurring in life without preconception, living in the present, and thinking with discernment and clarity.

The *Mindfulness Assessment* is designed to help you explore how mindful you currently are.

This assessment contains 24 statements related to how much you exhibit a mindful state. Read each of the statements and decide whether or not the statement describes you.

If the statement does describe you, circle the number next to that item in the YES column. If the statement does not describe you, circle the number next to that item in the NO column.

This is not a test.

There are no right or wrong answers.
Do not spend too much time thinking about your responses.

Be sure to respond to every statement.

(Continued on the next page)

Mindfulness Assessment

	YES	NO
I do things without thinking about them	1	2
I often forget how I arrived somewhere	1	2
I think before I react to stress	2	1
I have many biased notions about the world	1	2
I accept things just as they are	2	1
I notice things that happen each day	2	1

A.P. TOTAL = _____

I am aware of the various feelings in my body	2	1
I am unaware of many of the sounds around me	1	2
I am aware of my negative thoughts	2	1
I do not know what triggers my negative emotions	1	2
I do not feel unpleasant experiences in my body	1	2
I can distinguish between body and emotional sensations	2	1

P.L. TOTAL = _____

I spend a lot of time worrying about my past history	1	2
I live in the present a lot of the time	2	1
I can appreciate the present moment	2	1
I think way too much about the future	1	2
I pay attention to what is happening right now	2	1
When I am focused on the past, I can bring my awareness to now	2	1

P.M. TOTAL = _____

I am gentle with others	2	1
I judge my experiences as good or bad, nothing in between	1	2
I try not to judge the actions of others	2	1
I cannot bring my mind back into focus when it strays	1	2
I accept people for who and what they are	2	1
I often feel like a silent observer of my life	2	1

A.O. TOTAL = _____

Mindfulness Assessment

Scoring Directions

*For each of the four sections on the previous pages,
total the scores you circled and write them on the TOTAL line in each section. Then,
transfer your scores to the Individual Section Score column in the Table below.
Then add all four together and put that total in the "ALL 4" line below.*

Code	Section	The Goal	Individual Section Score
A.P.	Autopilot	Breaking away from being on autopilot all of the time.	
P.L.	Purposeful Life	Being more aware of yourself and your environment.	
P.M.	Present Moment	Staying in the present and not drifting into the past or the future.	
A.O.	Acceptance of Others	Seeing situations and people as they are and not judging them.	
ALL 4	TOTAL	**TOTAL OF ALL FOUR SECTIONS SCORE**	

Profile Interpretation for Individual Sections

Individual Sections	Score	Indications
11 to 12	High	You are a mindful person in the particular area in which you scored high. With additional practice, you can become even more mindful in this area.
8 to 10	Moderate	You are somewhat mindful in the particular area in which you scored moderate. With practice, you can become even more mindful.
6 to 7	Low	You are not very mindful at this point in time in the particular area in which you scored low. With practice, you can become much more mindful.

Profile Interpretation for All Four Sections

Total Sections	Score	Indications
36 to 48	High	You are a mindful person. With additional practice, you can become even more mindful.
25 to 35	Moderate	You are somewhat mindful. With practice, you can become even more mindful than you are right now.
12 to 24	Low	You are not very mindful at this point in time. With practice, you can become more mindful.

CHAPTER 1

Are You on Autopilot?

A BACKPACK OF MINDFULNESS TECHNIQUES

Throughout the "Are You on Autopilot?" chapter, you will find a variety of activity pages designed to help participants develop mindfulness attitudes and a mindful state of awareness.

As your participants complete an activity in this chapter, you may want to refer to Chapter Five, "Do You Have a Backpack of Mindfulness Techniques?" for practical tools and techniques that you can use to supplement and strengthen participant understanding of how to live a full life without being on autopilot.

Practitioner's Discussion Prior to Each Handout

The suggested discussions are written for groups; however, you can easily adapt them when you are working with an individual.

Chapter 1 – Are You on Autopilot?

What Are Your Daily Hassles? 22
   Tell the group that daily hassles are those little irritations that cause stress. Ask each person to name one of their daily hassles.

What are Your Difficult Hassles? 23
   Explain that a difficult hassle is any hassle that continues to make one's life difficult. Ask for volunteers to describe one of their difficult hassles. *Example: My back hurts and I cannot do some of the activities I would like to engage in.*

How Mindful Are You? 24
   Ask for volunteers to give a description of mindfulness. After they have had a chance to respond, share your own or this description - Mindfulness is an active state of mind when one engages in activities that are stimulating, fun, novel, and challenging. It is experienced when a sense of spirit fills one up with joy and wonderment or deep connectedness. It is a way to live without being on autopilot.

Are You Living on Autopilot? 25
   Ask the group participants, "What does it mean to be on autopilot?" Write their descriptors on the board for everyone to see. Provide an example of autopilot as realizing that one has driven oneself home, but hasn't really been paying attention. Then ask for other examples of being on autopilot.

What's Wearing You Down? 26
   Break participants into groups and ask participants to respond to each statement as TRUE or FALSE. Ask each group for their answer to each statement and then have a discussion based around each statement:
   - Daily hassles can wear you down over time (TRUE)
   - Daily hassles affect all people the same (FALSE)
   - Over time, stress from daily hassles wears people down (TRUE)
   - Daily hassles do not impact motivation and interest (FALSE)
   - Many go through life mindlessly and operate on autopilot rather than following their plans, interests, or desires (TRUE)

Are Your Old Habits Positive or Negative? 27
   Ask participants, "Why do people rely on old, familiar habits when times get stressful?"

How is Worry, Anxiety & Stress Effecting You? 28
   Remind participants that this handout is a quick assessment and not a test, and that the results are based solely on self-reported data provided by them. Also stress that nobody else will see their results, so they can be completely honest.

(Continued on the next page)

Practitioner's Discussion Prior to Each Handout *(Continued)*

Chapter 1 – Are You on Auto Pilot?

Can You Slow Down? 29
Ask group participants to describe the rate of speed at which they move through their lives. Ask for a volunteer to describe what makes his or her life so frantic. Describe the fact that in order to begin being more mindful in life, it is critical that one begins to slow down and live life more fully.

When Do You Zone Out? 30
Ask participants what zoning out means to them. *Example: Cutting off emotionally from everyone. Overlooking details. Forgetting.*

Do You Celebrate the Little Things? 31
Ask for volunteers to describe some of the big events or problems they are currently dealing with. Explain that focusing on big stuff can cause people to overlook some of the small things in life that are exciting and uplifting.

What are Two Daily Worries, Anxieties, and/or Stressors? 32
Ask for volunteers to mention something, big or little, that they worry about, feel anxious about, or stress about every day.

How Do You Start The Day? 33
Ask the group for a show of hands of those who felt that they were mindful in the morning opposed to just being on autopilot. Ask for volunteers to explain how that felt.

Do You Have a Restless Mind? 34
Ask for a show of hands for each of the following questions:
Tell participants that they can raise their hands for more than one.
 "Who are worriers?"
 "Who are logical and rationalize?"
 "Who are chatterers, with constant streams of thoughts going on?"
 "Who are distracters, jumping from one thing to another?"

Are You Comfortable Being with Yourself? 35
Explain that it is often difficult for people to be alone with themselves and just do nothing. They think things they don't want to think, rehash the day's hassles, and can't turn their minds off. Ask for volunteers to offer what people who feel like that tend to do. (*Example: Obsessively check the phone, email, social media, watch non-stop television, or keep themselves busy every moment in some way.*)

How Can You Become More Aware? 36
Tell participants that they can use their senses to become more aware. Ask for examples of how seeing, hearing, smelling, touching, tasting, watching body language, noticing verbal and nonverbal cues, etc. can ensure they are more aware.

What are Your Daily Hassles?

Negative life events *(Example: car accident, death of a loved one, moving to another location, etc.)* can be extremely stressful and can cloud every moment of the day. It is the daily hassles – those annoying or troublesome concerns – that cause enough worry, anxiety, and/or stress to wear people down over time.

Identify your daily hassles below by placing a check mark in front of the hassles that stress you out and then after each one that you check, describe why it is a daily hassle for you.

- ☐ Acceptance/Discrimination _____
- ☐ Accidents _____
- ☐ Body Language _____
- ☐ Dating _____
- ☐ Disagreements _____
- ☐ Environmental Issues _____
- ☐ Family _____
- ☐ Friends _____
- ☐ Future plans _____
- ☐ Gossip _____
- ☐ Job _____
- ☐ Laws _____
- ☐ Living space _____
- ☐ Loneliness _____
- ☐ Losing things _____
- ☐ Money _____
- ☐ Peer _____
- ☐ Physical and/or Mental Health _____
- ☐ Politics _____
- ☐ Pollution _____
- ☐ Responsibilities _____
- ☐ Rules _____
- ☐ School _____
- ☐ Sleep _____
- ☐ Social Media _____
- ☐ Technology _____
- ☐ Time _____
- ☐ To-Do list _____
- ☐ Transportation _____
- ☐ Unkindness _____
- ☐ Volunteer _____
- ☐ Waiting _____
- ☐ Other _____

What are Your Difficult Hassles?

It is important to be mindful and reflect on the hassles that seem difficult to you. Identifying them will help you to recognize when and why they are difficult, and to figure out how to cope with them.

Below, draw or doodle some of the difficult hassles in your life right now, why each is such a hassle, and think of how you can possibly deal with each one. (Example: It's my job to empty the dishwasher at home. It seems it always needs emptying when I am in a hurry. I can deal with it by remembering that the adults in our home do a lot for me and work hard to provide for us.)

"Problems are not stop signs, they are guidelines."
~ **Robert H. Schuller**

How Mindful are You?

Mindfulness is an active state of mind when you engage in activities that are stimulating, fun, novel, and challenging. It is experienced when a sense of spirit fills you up with joy and wonderment or deep connectedness. It is a way to live without being on autopilot and when you are able to be fully present. Living on autopilot means to do something without focusing on it or thinking about what is actually happening. Many people live their lives doing the same things over and over regardless of the results they receive. When this occurs, people lack awareness of what is occurring in their lives, and they operate from habit.

Respond to the questions below by journaling about your day yesterday to see how mindful you are.

- What time did you wake up in the morning?
- What did you eat for breakfast? Lunch? Dinner?
- What did you learn?
- With whom did you connect throughout the day?
- What was your most stressful moment and how did you feel?
- What was your most pleasant moment of the day and how did you feel?
- Who was kind to you? Explain.
- To whom were you kind? Explain.
- What made your day better?
- What did you do to make someone else's day better?
- How did your day end?
- What time did you go to sleep?

The more you remember about your day, the more mindful you tend to be. On a separate sheet of paper, pick one or two items and expand your reflections in detail.

Are You Living on Autopilot?

Many people live most of their lives on autopilot, not being aware that they are doing certain things. What types of things do you do without even thinking, while you are on autopilot? Some people drive and don't know which route they took and some people eat dinner without noticing the taste of the food.

Identify some of the things you do on autopilot, what you miss out on, and how you can be more mindful.

Ways I Am on Autopilot	What I Miss Out On	How I Can Be More Mindful
Example: On my phone I videoed something I thought would be interesting and wanted to capture it.	*I actually missed the moment because I was so busy trying to get the video focused just right.*	*I just should have appreciated the moment because I missed the experience and I may never go back to look at the video.*

"To be fully alive, fully human, and completely awake
is to be continually thrown out of the nest."
~ Pema Chödrön

What's Wearing You Down?

Over time, worry, anxiety, and/or stress from daily hassles wears people down and impacts their motivation and interest. They tend to start going through life mindlessly and operate on autopilot rather than their plans, interests, or desires.

In the boxes below, list ways the stress of daily hassles wears you down. Next to each one, problem-solve something you can do about it.

Example (inside of a box): My history teacher is boring and I just cannot absorb the materials.
Example (outside of the same box): I can form a study group of people with different learning styles to help each other out.

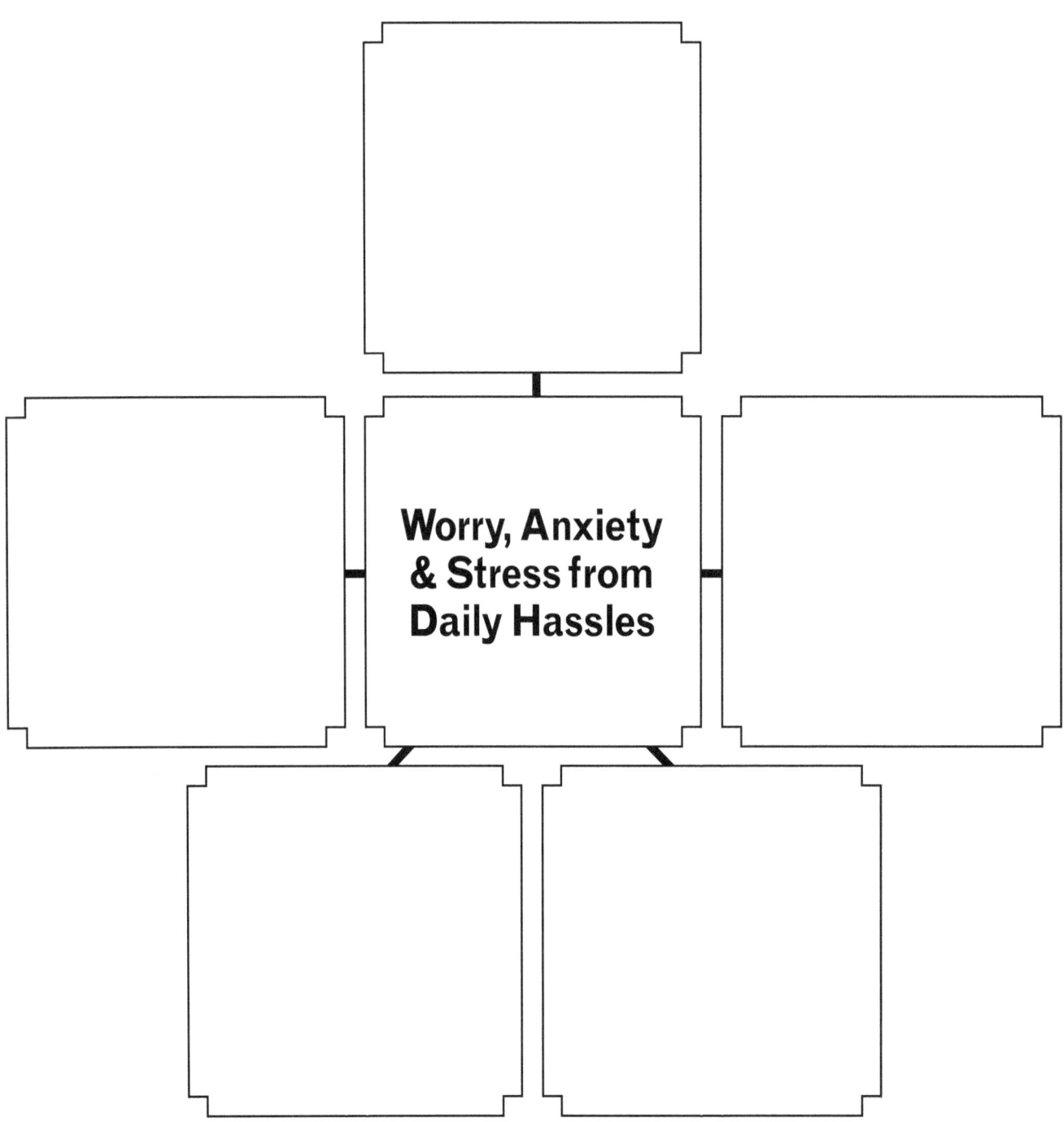

Are Your Old Habits Positive or Negative?

When people encounter enough worry, anxiety, and/or stress from daily hassles they lack energy and begin to rely on previous habits that have been formed – regardless of whether these habits are positive or negative. This autopilot can keep people from living a satisfying, more stimulating and worthwhile life based on values, purpose, and meaning.

Identify the times when you go back to the old habits you have formed in the past. Identify if these habits are positive or negative, and describe their effect on you.

Old Habits	Positive or Negative	Ways it Affects Me
Example: I become worried why my friends do not respond to my social media posts.	☐ *Positive* ☑ *Negative*	*I feel anxious and think that they don't care enough about me to respond.*
	☐ *Positive* ☐ *Negative*	
	☐ *Positive* ☐ *Negative*	
	☐ *Positive* ☐ *Negative*	
	☐ *Positive* ☐ *Negative*	
	☐ *Positive* ☐ *Negative*	
	☐ *Positive* ☐ *Negative*	
	☐ *Positive* ☐ *Negative*	

How is Worry, Anxiety & Stress Effecting You?

It is important to explore how much you are living on autopilot and experiencing worry, anxiety, and/or stress from all of the daily hassles you encounter in life.

- The statements below represent ways people experience worry, anxiety, and/or stress.
- For each of the statements listed below, identify if the statement is like you or not.
- If the statement is like you, circle the number under the LIKE ME column.
- If the statement is not like you, circle the number under the NOT LIKE ME column.

	LIKE ME	NOT LIKE ME
I feel exhausted by the end of my day	1	2
I feel as if I am always rushing to get something done	1	2
I cannot relax even when I have nothing I need to do	1	2
I multi-task and seem to get nothing done right	1	2
I find myself "zoning out"	1	2
I feel run down and I lack energy	1	2
I cannot motivate myself even to do the things I like	1	2
I am often impatient with other people	1	2
I do many things without even knowing I am doing them	1	2
I have difficulty operating at a slow pace	1	2

TOTAL = _____

To score the assessment you just completed:
- Count the numbers you circled for each of the ten items above.
- Put that total on the line marked TOTAL.
- Next look at the interpretation guide below to see what your score means.
- Your score will be between 10 and 20.

- If you scored between 10 and 13: you are experiencing a great deal of worry, anxiety, and/or stress related to your daily hassles.
- If you scored between 14 and 17: you are experiencing some worry, anxiety, and/or stress related to your daily hassles.
- If you scored between 18 and 20: you are not experiencing much worry, anxiety, and/or stress related to your daily hassles.

Can You Slow Down?

In order to begin being more mindful, it is critical that you begin to slow down and live life more deliberately, mindfully, and purposefully. To do this, you need to begin being more mindful about the activities toward which you do not ordinarily pay much attention.

Below, list your daily routines (eating meals, skateboarding, doing chores, driving, etc.) and describe how you can be more intentional when engaged in them.

My Routine Activities	How I Typically do This	How I Can be More Mindful and Intentional
Example: Walking to school.	*I take the same route to school every day.*	*I can take different routes, observe the various businesses and look for a summer job.*

Which types of activities are you least mindful about? Why?

_____

_____

_____

_____

When Do You Zone Out?

When people live on autopilot they often zone out during the day and do things without being aware that they are doing them. Notice where and when you tend to zone out. *(Example: driving, sitting in a classroom, emailing or texting, web surfing, feeding the dog, doing homework, watching television, brushing teeth, etc.).*

Practice bringing more awareness to activities by filling in the following statements by journaling, drawing, or doodling your responses:

I zone out when...
Example: In the classroom.

I can become more aware by...
Example: Focus on what the teacher is saying.

I zone out when...

I can become more aware by...

I zone out when...

I can become more aware by...

Do You Celebrate the Little Things?

People often think too much about the big things that occur in their everyday lives. This can cause them to overlook some of the small things in life that are exciting and uplifting. Use your tablet, cellphone, or pad and pencil to jot down the little things you notice during your day.

Example: Someone held a door open for you; you held the door for another person; you made friends with someone culturally different from you; you helped someone with homework; you told a friend how much you appreciated them; it rained all week and today the sun is shining!

List, draw, or write a poem about some of the little things you did yesterday or today that can be celebrated. Then, share your celebrations with others!

What are Two Daily Worries, Anxieties, and/or Stressors?

By becoming aware of your daily worries, anxieties, and/or stressors you can begin to be aware of how they affect you, your actions, and reactions. Then explain if and how this perpetuates the stress.

My Daily Worry, Anxiety, and/or Stressor #1: _____
_____
_____

My actions: _____
_____

My reactions: _____
_____

How do these reactions help or how do they perpetuate the worry, anxiety, and/or stress? _____
_____

What can I do about it? _____
_____
_____

My Daily Worry, Anxiety, and/or Stressor #2: _____=
_____
_____

My actions: _____
_____

My reactions: _____
_____

How do these reactions help or how do they perpetuate the worry, anxiety, and/or stress? _____
_____

What can I do about it? _____
_____
_____

How Do You Start The Day?

It is SO helpful to get off to a good start in the morning by being mindful of what is happening within you and what is occurring in your environment. To do so, you need to start each day with a positive, calm state of mind.

Respond to the following questions to explore your wake-up routine.

What or who wakes you up? _____
_____

What do you do?
  ☐ Jump out of bed?
  ☐ Snooze?
  ☐ Go back to sleep?
  ☐ Depend on someone to wake you again?

What is your routine once you are out of bed? _____
_____
_____
_____

What is your getting dressed routine? _____
_____
_____
_____

What is your breakfast routine? _____
_____
_____
_____

Do you start the morning texting, emailing, checking social media, and/or surfing the Internet? _____
  • If so, how much time do you spend doing this? _____
  • How does that affect your conversations with others? _____
  • How does that affect your mood as you begin your day? _____
  • How does that affect you as you go through the day? _____

Do you go on with the next part of the day feeling relaxed? Explain. _____
_____

Do you go on with the next part of the day feeling rushed? Explain. _____
_____

Do You Have a Restless Mind?

People often listen to their self-talk even when their mind is providing bad advice. There are many restless ways that the mind keeps people from being mindful and filled with worry, anxiety, and/or stress.

For each type of self-talk your mind provides, list your experiences and their affects.

Worrier
(Worries about everything)

Rationalizer
(Uses logic)

Chatterer
(Constant stream of thoughts)

Distractor
(Jumping from one thing to another)

After looking over your comments, what can you try to do differently?

_____

_____

Mindfulness allows people to shut their minds down and focus on the experience by staying in the present and being non-judgmental.

Are You Comfortable Being with Yourself?

It is often difficult for people to be with themselves and do nothing. Many people are quite afraid of being alone with themselves because their mind goes wondering on autopilot, and the process often becomes a negative one. They think things they don't want to think, rehash the day's hassles, and can't turn their thoughts off. To avoid this, they obsessively check the phone, email, social media, watch non-stop television, or keep themselves busy in some way.

Identify some of the ways that you distract yourself by staying busy.

Ways I Distract Myself	How It Affects Me	How I Can Avoid This and Be More Comfortable With Me
Example: I keep checking my phone.	It makes me feel important if someone is reaching out to me but it makes me feel unimportant if there are no messages.	Put my cell phone away for at least an hour every few hours.

This is where mindfulness comes in to make all the difference in the world!

How Can You Become More Aware?

Being able to identify your thoughts, feelings, and environment is an easy first step to developing awareness and becoming more mindful of what you are doing during the day. Rather than drifting off into autopilot, take note of everything that is going on around you. The next time you are going somewhere, notice every sign you pass, building you see, the beauty of nature around you, people's faces and body language, and be aware of the distances between you and other people and vehicles.

Get together with another person. Each one of you will need a copy of this page. You will each pick three of your routine activities, and journal about how you feel when you are mindful compared to the days when you do the activity on autopilot. Write about it and then take turns describing to each other what you wrote.

One of My Routine Activities	How I Feel When I Do It On Autopilot	How I Experience It When I Do It Mindfully
Example: Riding my bike to school in the morning.	I just keep going the same route without noticing anything unusual.	I notice the trees, the flowers in bloom, the lady who lives down the block walking her poodle, Mr. Jones picking up his newspaper, etc.

#1 – My Routine Activity	How I Feel When I Do It On Autopilot	How I Experience It When I Do It Mindfully

#2 – My Routine Activity	How I Feel When I Do It On Autopilot	How I Experience It When I Do It Mindfully

#3 – My Routine Activity	How I Feel When I Do It On Autopilot	How I Experience It When I Do It Mindfully

Quotes about Autopilot

On the lines that follow, describe what each of these quotes mean to you and how they apply to YOUR life.

"Get in the driver's seat of your thoughts. You control them
and they absolutely control your life."
~ **Sam Owen**

_____
_____
_____
_____
_____

"Very often, human beings are living like on autopilot, reacting automatically with what happens. What interests me about the life of an explorer is you are in the unknown; you are out of your habits."
~ **Bertrand Piccard**

_____
_____
_____
_____
_____

"Life is not a journey you want to make on autopilot."
~ **Paula Rinehart**

_____
_____
_____
_____
_____

CHAPTER 2

Do You Pay Full Attention?

> **A BACKPACK OF MINDFULNESS TECHNIQUES**
>
> Throughout the "Do You Pay Full Attention?" chapter, you will find a variety of activity pages designed to help participants develop mindfulness attitudes toward living a purposeful life.
>
> As your participants complete an activity in this chapter, you may want to refer to Chapter Five, "Do You Have a Backpack of Mindfulness Techniques?" for practical tools and techniques that you can use to supplement and strengthen participant understanding of how to live a full purposeful life.

Practitioner's Discussion Prior to Each Handout

The suggested discussions are written for groups; however, you can easily adapt them when you are working with an individual.

Chapter 2 – Do You Pay Full Attention?

Does Your Mind Wander? 44
Ask participants to share information about the times when their minds wander.

Can You Control Your Focus? 45
Explain to participants that focus can be disrupted by internal forces such as wanting to be somewhere else or thinking about being somewhere else, and by external forces such as cell phones going off. Ask them for their own examples.

Do You Get Caught Up In Your Feelings? 46
Provide some examples of the various ways people can get caught up in the feelings related to daily hassles. Ask participants to identify a daily hassle and the feelings connected with that hassle.

Are You Aware of Your Actions? 47
Explain to participants that mindfulness and awareness are very similar, but not the same. Being aware of having to do something is very different from being mindful of how you are doing it. Mindfulness is paying attention even while in the midst of an everyday hassle. Ask them to brainstorm ways they are mindful and ways they are aware.

Do You Bring Purpose to What You Do? 48
Ask participants to identify several daily tasks which are a hassle. Explain that by paying mindful attention to these tasks, they can change them from hassles to having a mindful purpose. One example might be feeding dog. Take time to interact with the dog before and after he eats, showing him he is loved.

Are You Aware of Being Mindful? 49
Explain that in order to develop mindfulness, people need to make a commitment to slow their life down, take responsibility for their actions, and become more aware of their thoughts, feelings, and actions. Ask participants to pair up and describe one way in which they will slow down and take more responsibility.

How Do You React to Worry, Anxiety, and Stress? 50
Discuss with the group that people react differently to worry, anxiety, and stress. Explain that knowing when and how they experience this thinking will help them to recognize when they are at risk, in crisis, and acting or reacting in a way of which they would not be proud.

What is Your Habitual Reaction? 51
Talk about the fact that different people react to the same situation in different ways. Ask participants to share how they usually react when they are extremely angry.

(Continued on the next page)

Practitioner's Discussion Prior to Each Handout *(Continued)*

Chapter 2 – Do You Pay Full Attention?

Do You Engage in "What If..." Thinking? 52
Ask group participants what "What if..." thinking is. After some discussion, describe "What if... thinking" as "When the mind naturally wanders to the future, people often forget about thinking about the present." Ask for some examples.

Do You Pay Full Attention? 53
Share with the participants that paying full attention means becoming attuned to their thoughts, emotions, physical reactions, reactions to sounds, and other disturbances. Ask for some examples.

What Are Your Internal Forces? 54
Ask the group, "What is an Internal Force?" (Internal forces are those distractions occurring within you and the context of your body and mind.) Have participants identify internal forces that take their attention away from the present: desires (hunger), motivations (to be the best at something) and urges (to stay up watching television all night) that intercept our attention to the present.

What Are Your External Forces? 55
Ask the group, "What is an External Force?" (External forces are those distractions that are occurring outside of you and in your environment.) Ask participants to identify the many external forces that take their attention away from the present including desires (to live in another neighborhood), motivations (pressure placed to be more productive), and urges (to be swimming rather than where you are right now), that intercept our attention to the present.

Are You Aware of Your Mental State? 56
Remind participants that awareness of one's own mental state is a critical aspect in developing mindfulness. Paying attention means developing a habit of observing one's mental state at this moment. Ask for volunteers to share their mental state in one word.

Can You Change the Moment? 57
Write the word "present" on the board. Suggest to participants that attention and focus can be used to decrease their negative thinking and change the way they feel. They can change the moment by deliberately changing their focus of attention. Ask participants to notice the judgments their mind is making at this very moment and ask them to change their emotion by saying to themselves that it is not so bad. Notice how your feelings change? Discuss this in the group.

Do You Take Time to Smell The Roses? 58
Ask people if they get so caught up in the day-to-day hustle and bustle of their everyday lives that they forget to pay attention to, and enjoy, the small things in life such as a beautiful ocean, the smell of fresh-baked bread, or their favorite song. Ask each person to "smell the roses" and tell about something that is special that they might have overlooked today.

Does Your Mind Wander?

Your mind can naturally wander and take your focus from the present pursuit or task at hand. When your mind wanders, it may cause worry, anxiety, and stress. It is important to be intentional when thinking about tasks you have ahead of you by making a conscientious effort to focus on the specific tasks and not allow your mind to wander.

Below, pick three of your current to-do tasks and describe how your mind wanders and how you can bring your attention back to what you are doing in the present.

My number one task is...

The ways my mind wanders are...

I can bring my mind back by...

The projected outcome is...

My number two task is...

The ways my mind wanders are...

I can bring my mind back by...

The projected outcome is...

My number three task is...

The ways my mind wanders are...

I can bring my mind back by...

The projected outcome is...

Can You Control Your Focus?

Being able to control your focus with all of the distractions, hassles, worries, anxiety, and stress going on outside of you *(friends calling, television, lost keys, going to a class you dislike, etc.)* or within you *(wanting to be somewhere else, worrying about college applications, etc.)* is the first step in having the ability to focus on what is going on with you in the present, right now! It is important to notice (be mindful) when your mind wanders, and when it does, focus on bringing your attention back to what you choose to fully pay attention to. You can say FOCUS to yourself to bring your attention back.

Below, identify how your mind wanders, whether it is outside of you and/or within you, and how you can bring your attention back into focus.

When My Mind Wanders	My Mind Wanders Because of Things Outside of Me	My Mind Wanders Because of Things or Within Me	How I Will Focus to Bring Back My Attention
Example: In a class	I am worried about not getting a scholarship to the college I hope to attend.		I will learn to be aware of what I can control. I have sent in all of my scholarship application materials and I tried my best.
Example: In a class		I become anxious when I have to get up in front of the class and do presentations.	I will say FOCUS to myself and concentrate on what is being said at the moment, and not focus on my presentation.

Do You Get Caught Up in Negative Feelings?

It's easy to get caught up in negative feelings of worry, anxiety, and/or stress about the hassles of the day. *(Example: personal relationships, school, peers, social media, family drama, etc.)* However, you can adopt the skills of focusing only on the topics that you need to think about.

Name a situation when you tend most often to allow your negative feelings to interfere with your actions.

_____
_____
_____

Does this situation cause you worry, anxiety, and/or stress, or all three? Explain

_____
_____
_____

Draw or write about the situation you described above.

I get caught up in my negative feelings when…	When I do, I usually…
The effect of this is usually…	**I can get my feelings under control by…**

Are You Always Aware of Your Actions?

Mindfulness and awareness are very similar, but not the same. Being aware you must do something is very different from being mindful of how you are doing it. Mindfulness is paying attention even while in the midst of an everyday hassle.

Below, explore the times when you are aware that you need to do things, and do them without thinking about them, and then compare it with those times you are mindful about doing something.

Times I do something mindlessly, just to do it and get it over with!	Times I am mindful about something every moment I am doing it!
Example: When I am asked by a member of my family for help fixing their computer, I just fix it quickly but do not show them how to fix it themselves.	*Example: When I volunteer at the dog shelter, I am careful when walking and feeding the dogs... they need my love and attention.*

"The key to growth is the introduction of higher dimensions of consciousness into our awareness."
~ **Lao Tzu**

Do You Bring Purpose to What You Do?

By paying attention to what you are doing and where you are focused, you give what you do purpose. By being present, staying in the moment, and focusing your attention you bring purpose to everything you do.

(Example: When working on an art project, the purpose is being aware and paying attention to the art materials, the feel of them, and the way they could go together to form something wonderful, such as designing a hooked rug: choose colors, materials, size, design, etc.)

This awareness and attention can help you to identify the purpose of your actions. It can help you to find purpose in the daily hassles in your life.

Below, identify several daily tasks which are a hassle, how you can attend to these tasks, and how attending to them can help you find purpose in them.

Task #1

Attention:

Purpose:

Task #2

Attention:

Purpose:

Task #3

Attention:

Purpose:

Are You Aware of Being Mindful?

Awareness is one of the key elements of being mindful. In developing mindfulness, people make a commitment to slow their life down *(Example: Join fewer clubs)*, take responsibility for their actions *(Example: Complete chores)*, and to become more aware of their thoughts, feelings, and actions *(Example: Start a reflective journal)*. These are the keystones to mindfulness.

Journal about how you will commit to being more attentive.

Slow Down	I will
Slow Down	I will
Slow Down	I will
Slow Down	I will

Take Responsibility	I will
Take Responsibility	I will
Take Responsibility	I will
Take Responsibility	I will

Be Self-Aware	I will
Be Self-Aware	I will
Be Self-Aware	I will
Be Self-Aware	I will

How Do You React to Worry, Anxiety & Stress?

Most of the time people are unaware of how much worry, anxiety, and stress they are experiencing, and they do not realize how out-of-touch they are with themselves. Knowing when and how you experience negative thinking related to worry, anxiety, and/or stress will help you to recognize when you are at risk, in crisis, or acting (or reacting) in a way that you would not be proud of.

Identify times when you feel worry, anxiety, and/or stress.

Situations and Times When I Feel Worry, Anxiety, or Stress	Ways I React When I Feel Worry, Anxiety, or Stress	Symptoms I Have When I Feel Worry, Anxiety, or Stress	Thoughts I Experience When I Feel Worry, Anxiety, or Stress
Example: When I need to speak in front of other people in one of my classes.	My mind goes blank	I get nervous and sweaty	I start to think about how awful it will be if I mess up!

"The truth is that there is no actual stress or anxiety in the world; it's your thoughts that create these false beliefs. You can't package stress, touch it, or see it. There are only people engaged in stressful thinking."
~ Wayne Dyer

What is Your Habitual Reaction?

When we encounter daily hassles, and symptoms of worry, anxiety, and stress, our reactions can be subtle or strong. The reality is that most people tend to react in very different ways to the daily stressors they encounter. Think about when you encounter daily hassles in your life, and describe how you tend to react using the descriptors that follow. You may write about a variety of hassles, and how they worry you, cause you anxiety, and/or increase your level of stress.

Write about the ways you usually react and about the circumstances surrounding your reactions.

I freeze and don't know how to react when…

I eat when…

I panic when…

I am extremely anxious when…

I become angry when…

I withdraw and get very quiet when…

I busy myself with other things when…

I blame others when…

I feel hurt when…

My body feels tense when…

Do You Engage in "What If" Thinking?

Without realizing it, many people pay more attention to the future than to the present. When too focused on the future, people worry about things that may never happen, feel anxious, stress out about it, and lose focus on the present. They often do this by making predictions about where they will be or what they will be doing tomorrow, next week, next month, next year, and further in the future. This often takes the form of "What if..." thinking. When the mind naturally wanders to the future, people often forget to think about the present.

Identify those times when your mind makes "What if..." predictions about the future.

My "What If..." Predictions	How it Affects Me	How It Affects My Present Tasks and Situations
Example: What if I don't get the part-time job I want?	I spend more time worrying about this than on the work I need to be doing now.	My grades are falling off.
Example: What if I don't get the part-time job I want?	I will have more time to spend on finding a better job than the one I didn't get.	I will work on my grades to better position myself.

How is Your Attention Span?

What is one of your daily hassles? _____

_____

How does this cause you worry, anxiety, and/or stress? _____

_____

_____

As you think about this hassle and the worry, anxiety, and/or stress it causes, turn your full attention to what is going on inside of you. Write or illustrate your experiences.

Thoughts	**Reactions to sounds and other disturbances**
Emotions	**Physical reactions**

What are Your INTERNAL Forces?

Many internal forces take our attention away from the present. We experience various wants, needs, and motivations that intercept our attention to the present. These types of internal forces can be strong and destructive.

Identify your wants (example: to play video games until two in the morning) **that keep you from paying attention to tasks,** *needs* (example: hunger), **and** *motivations* (example: to be the best student in the class).

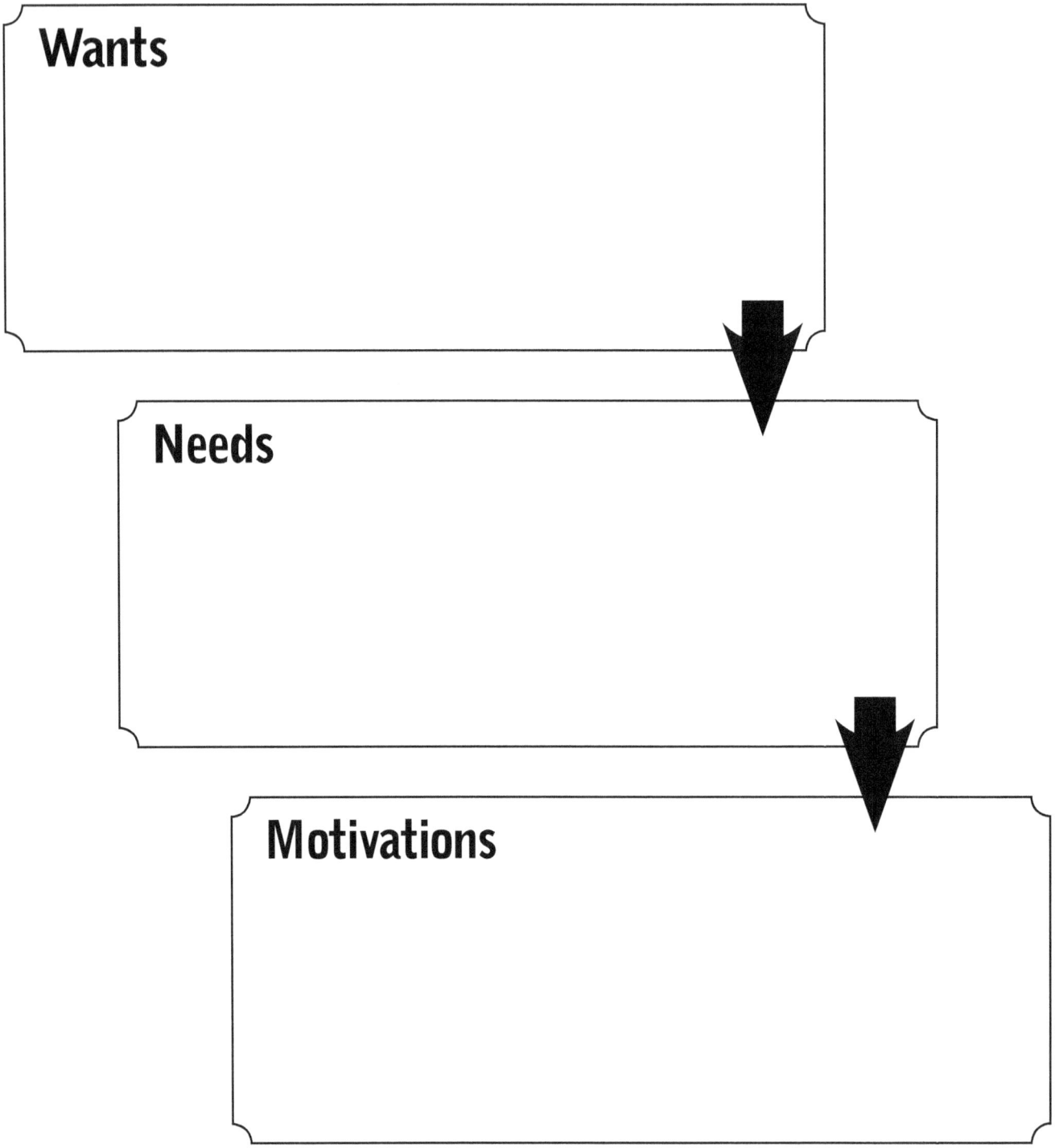

What are Your EXTERNAL Forces?

Many external forces take our attention away from the present. We experience various wants, needs, and motivations that intercept our attention to the present. These types of external forces can be strong and destructive.

*Identify your **wants** (example: play rather than work), **needs** (example: being outside when it's good weather), **and motivations** (example: the weather is perfect to go hiking rather than work).*

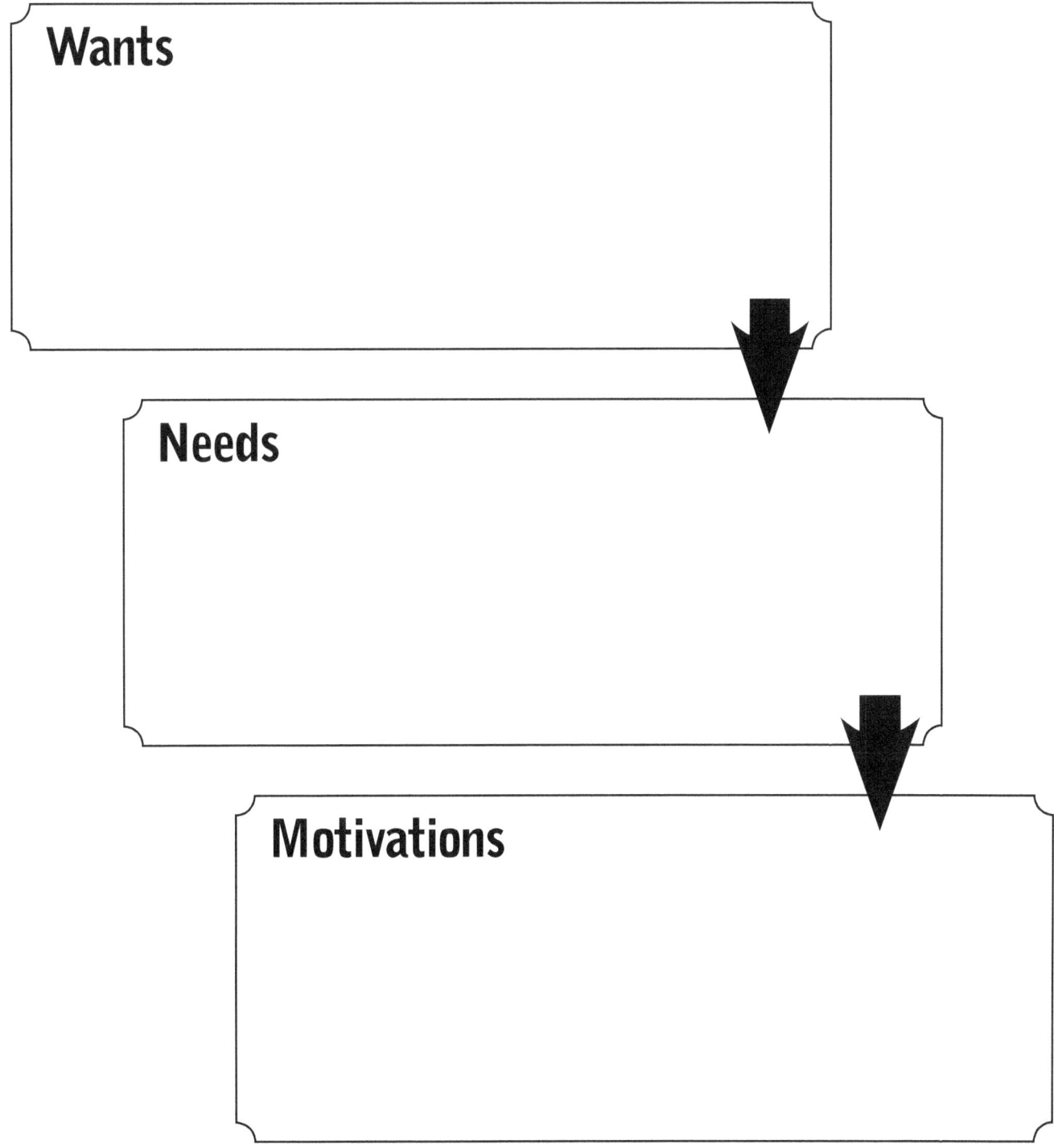

Are You Aware of Your Mental State?

Awareness of your mental state is a critical aspect in developing mindfulness. Paying attention means developing a habit of observing the mental states that arise in the mind. Various mental states will take you from the present into the past and/or into the future, thus keeping you from paying full attention to what you are currently doing. Write about two of your most intrusive thoughts in the box on the left. In the middle box explain how that interferes with your ability to be aware, and then why you need to let the thought go. *(Example: I keep thinking that if I grew up in a different family my life would be better, I keep feeling sorry for myself, and I know I cannot change how I grew up).*

Intruding Thoughts from the Past

My Intruding Thought from the Past	How It Interferes with My Awareness	Why I Need to Let The Thought Go

Intruding Thoughts about the Future

My Intruding Thought about the Future	How It Interferes with My Awareness	Why I Need to Let The Thought Go

A Secret about Successful Mindfulness

One of the secrets about mindfulness is to avoid becoming involved in thoughts as they arise, by simply observing them from a distance, taking a few deep breaths, and dismissing them. If a thought arises that is very strong, then the option is to be aware of it, take a few deep breaths, accept its presence, but still stay detached from it. Once you feel more able to deal with the thought because you have stepped back from it, you can then let go of the thought, or turn your attention to the thought. You can ask yourself "Is this thought useful or is it causing me stress?" Then let it go.

Now you try it and journal about what you discover.

_____

_____

_____

Can You Change the Moment?

Attention and focus are very important because they can be used to decrease your problematic thinking and change the way you manage your worry, anxiety, and/or stress. You can change the moment by deliberately changing your focus of attention. One good strategy is to notice the judgments your mind is making and use this information to change your emotions. Try this method with one of your daily hassles.

One of my daily hassles: _____

_____

_____

Does this hassle cause worry, anxiety, and/or stress? Why? _____

What were you thinking as you wrote about this hassle? _____

_____

_____

_____

Describe what you are feeling in your body: _____

_____

_____

_____

How does this daily hassle interfere with what you want and need? _____

_____

_____

Name and describe your emotion(s) when you think about it: _____

_____

_____

How can you refocus your thinking in a positive way to change the emotion(s) you are experiencing? __

_____

_____

This process allows you to be in control rather than being controlled by outside events.

Do You Take Time to Smell The Roses?

People get caught up in the day-to-day hassles that ultimately cause worry, anxiety and/or stress, that they forget to pay attention to and enjoy the small things in life like the aroma of fresh baked cookies, the vivid green color of a football field, or the warmth of the sun on your face. The saying "smell the roses" is about deliberately noticing the things that you overlook every day.

Identify those people, tasks, and things you overlook but want to begin to pay more attention.

People, Tasks & Things I Tend to Overlook	How and Why I Overlook Them	How I Can Pay More Attention
Example: My friends always seem to be there for me with full support when I need them.	I take them for granted and assume that they will always be available to me.	I will start telling them how I appreciate each of them and make sure that I, in turn, am supportive of them.

"Today, just take time to smell the roses, enjoy those little things about your life, your family, spouse, friends, job. Forget about the thorns — the pains and problems they cause you — and enjoy life."
~ **Bernard Kelvin Clive**

Quotes about Paying Attention

In the spaces that follow, describe what each of the quotes mean to you and how they apply to your life.

"Pay attention to the little things. They're more important than you may think."
~ **Matt Gutierrez**

_____
_____
_____
_____
_____
_____
_____
_____
_____

"I just sit back and observe. You learn more that way."
~ **Sonya Teclai**

_____
_____
_____
_____
_____
_____
_____
_____
_____

CHAPTER 3

Can You Stay in the Present Moment?

A BACKPACK OF MINDFULNESS TECHNIQUES

Throughout the "Can You Stay in the Present Moment?" chapter, you will find a variety of activity pages designed to help participants develop mindfulness attitudes toward living in the present moment.

As your participants complete an activity in this chapter, you may want to refer to Chapter Five, "Do You Have a Backpack of Mindfulness Techniques?" for practical tools and techniques that you can use to supplement and strengthen participant understanding of how to focus and live in the present.

Practitioner's Discussion Prior to Each Handout

The suggested discussions are written for groups; however, you can easily adapt them when you are working with an individual.

Chapter 3 – Do You Live in the Present Moment?

Do You Tend to Focus on the Present or the Past? 66
Explain to the group that although the past is gone, it is very easy to get hung up on hassles and problems that have happened in the past. Ask for a show of hands of participants who spend a good deal of time dwelling on incidents and people from their past. Allow participants to debate this question: "How do you know if you are spending too much time dwelling on the past?"

How is Your Breath a Gift? 67
Ask the participants why quotations from wise people can be beneficial. Some possibilities below:
- They can help you reflect on your life for meaning and purpose.
- They can be transformative.
- They can alter the way you think about certain situations.
- They can provide optimism and hope.
- They can help you to become the best version of yourself.
- They can inspire you to reach for new goals.

Do You Learn Your Lesson? 68
Explain that one way to stop focusing on the worries, anxieties, and stressors from the past is to identify and explore why your mind strays into the past. Ask for volunteers to share when their minds stray to the past. If they wish, they can explain why that happens.

Do You Go with the Flow? 69
Ask participants what it means to "go with the flow." Now ask for volunteers: "Tell about a time when you or someone else went with the flow and it worked out well?" Then ask, "What is a time when you or someone else did NOT go with the flow and it worked out well?"

Do You Get Caught up in the Future? 70
Explain that many people focus on the future, not the present. Ask for volunteers to give an example to this question: How has focusing too much on the future caused you to worry, to experience anxiety, and/or to feel stressed?

Are Your Routines Becoming TOO Routine? 71
Ask for responses from participants. "Are regular routines good or bad? Why?" After some discussion explain that routines do make life easier; however, when you are stuck in a routine, you are usually not being mindful of all that is around you. You can do something as simple as changing the way that you drive to work, varying what you wear, listening to different music, finding a new friend very different from you, or trying a hobby you have never tried.

(Continued on the next page)

Practitioner's Discussion Prior to Each Handout *(Continued)*

Chapter 3 – Do You Live in the Present Moment?

How "Should" You Be? 72
Ask participants what they believe Victoria Moran was saying: "In this moment, there is plenty of time. In this moment, you are precisely as you should be. In this moment, there is infinite possibility."

Do You Multi-Task or Uni-Task? 73
Break the participants into two groups. Assign one group the task of brainstorming ways that multi-tasking is good, and assign the other group the task of brainstorming ways that uni-tasking is good. Then allow them to debate which is better. Afterwards, explain that there are occasions when both approaches might work best, but that a mindful approach is critical.

Can You Slow Down, You Crazy Child? 74
Prior to distributing the handouts, ask participants to describe what they hear in this Paul Simon song lyric, "Slow down, you move too fast. You gotta make the morning last." Explain that moving too fast in life means jumping from one activity to another without being fully present and focusing and enjoying each activity!

Do You Think Too Much? 75
Ask for a show of hands of people who believe they think too much. Explain that this means that while they are supposedly doing something else, they are thinking about an annoying neighbor, the future, the past, what's for dinner, why the darn dog is loose again, or what they want to do this weekend.

Remind participants that this can be harmful in many ways:
- They are not present in what they are doing and may make mistakes.
- They can't fully appreciate what is happening right now.
- They miss out on things.
- They are unable to enjoy the process of whatever they are engaged in.

Are You Present When Listening? 76
Ask participants to raise hands for each of the statements that they believe to be true of themselves.
- I give others my full attention without letting my mind wander.
- I listen for the meaning behind the words of the other person.
- I maintain good eye contact without staring.
- I make a conscious effort to find ways to remain present when speaking with others.
- I mindfully pay attention to what the other person is saying.
- I mirror and reflect what I hear the other person saying.
- I pay attention to how I feel as the other person speaks.
- I refrain from searching for a response while others are speaking.
- I show interest and appropriate body language.
- I tune out distractions to my conversations.

With the group, discuss which of the statements is the most difficult to do when engaged in a conversation.

Do You Tend to Focus on the Present or the Past?

It is very easy to get hung up on hassles and problems that have happened in the past. Many people live most of their current lives dwelling on incidents, friends, etc., from their past. When people do this, their ability to be mindful in the present, appreciating all of the goodness around them, is diminished. The present is the only place that can be free from worry, anxiety, and stress. The fact is, nothing that happened can change; we can only learn from it.

In each box, list a situation in which you find your mind focusing on the past, rather than staying in the present.

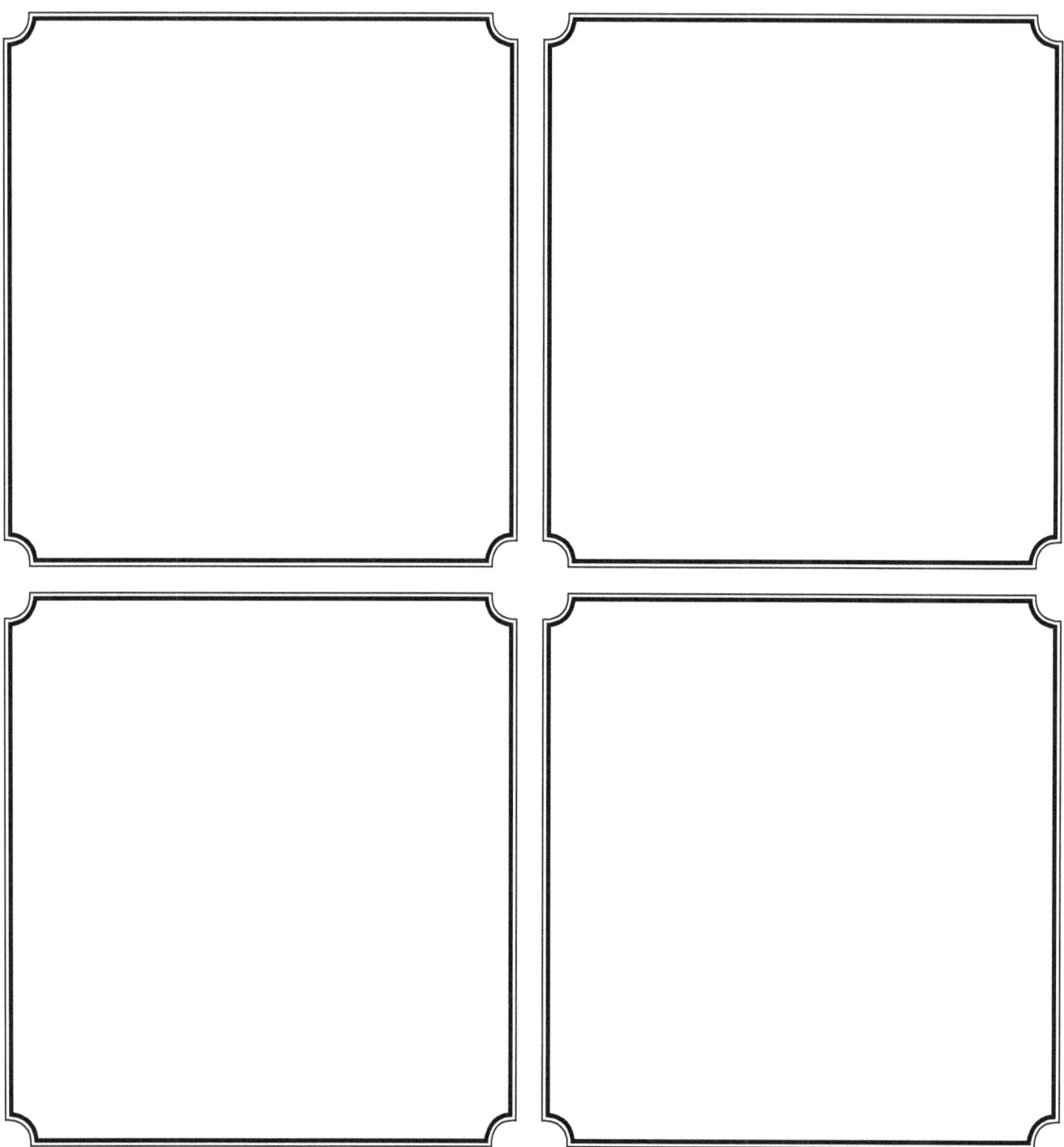

How is Your Breath a Gift?

"Living in the moment means letting go of the past and not waiting for the future. It means living your life consciously, aware that each moment you breathe is a gift."
~ Oprah Winfrey

How does the quotation above pertain to you? _____
_____
_____
_____

Name three hassles from your past that you might want (and need) to let go.

1. _____
2. _____
3. _____

Name the advantages of your dwelling on these hassles. (Respond to corresponding hassle numbers above.)

1. _____
2. _____
3. _____

Name the disadvantages of your dwelling on these hassles. (Respond to corresponding hassle numbers above.)

1. _____
2. _____
3. _____

Re-read the Oprah Winfrey quotation and write how you might live your life being aware that *each moment you breathe is a gift*.

_____
_____
_____
_____

Do You Learn Your Lesson?

One way to stop focusing on the worries, anxieties, and stressors from the past is to identify and explore why your mind strays into the past. You can achieve this by remembering that you can learn life-changing lessons from these experiences, without dwelling on them. By doing this, you break the hold that your past has on you and you can more easily stay in the present.

Explore your past incidents, why you continue to focus on them, and lessons you learned from each one.

Incidents from My Past	What Was the Result	What I Learned From It
Example: I was angry at my friend for not helping me get a job where she works.	She refused to see me for over two years. I was devastated.	I learned that we all are not perfect, I need to learn to forgive others, and find a way to reconnect with her again.

What do these words mean to you?

Stay present for the "now" in your life. It's your point of power.

Do You Go with the Flow?

Every moment of our lives we have the possibility of being totally involved and engaged. Often, people forgo a present moment to think about what is coming next. When this occurs, people lose their "being in the moment," and begin to experience worry, anxiety, and/or stress about the next day or week, or years ahead.

Explore the activities that have you so absorbed that time disappears and you are totally present. In the spaces that follow, describe some of the ways you find yourself in the flow of life and some ways you can do this more often.

Example: I'm in the flow when I... Sing	*I can feel this more often by...* *I can join a choir, and possibly major in music in college.*
I'm in the flow when I...	I can feel this more often by...
I'm in the flow when I...	I can feel this more often by...
I'm in the flow when I...	I can feel this more often by...
I'm in the flow when I...	I can feel this more often by...

How can you bring flow to more of your activities?

_____

_____

_____

Do You Get Caught Up in the Future?

It is important to plan and set goals for your future. However, when you focus so much on them that they cause worry, anxiety, and/or stress, and begin to affect your daily life, it can become a problem. Practicing mindfulness means keeping your attention focused solely in the present moment.

Identify goals for your future and describe how you will not allow yourself to get caught up in worrying about what may or may not happen. These worries about the future keep you from being in the present!

Goals for My Future	How I Will NOT Get Caught Up Worrying
Example: Bring up my grade point average in school.	*I will work very hard, do my homework, and do my best. However, I am determined to not obsess over it.*

Are Your Routines Becoming TOO Routine?

The reason people often do NOT live in the present moment is that they are set in a certain routine and do the things in that routine without conscious awareness. One way to become aware and more present is to change up some of your routines. You can do something as simple as changing the route where you walk your dog, varying what you wear, listening to different music, finding a new friend very different from you, or trying a hobby you have never tried. Making a small change to a couple of your routines may be enough to make you more aware of your surroundings.

Draw pictures, doodle, or write about some new routines that might appeal to you.

Early Morning	School

Friendships	Time in Nature

How "Should" You Be?

"In this moment, there is plenty of time. In this moment, you are precisely as you should be. In this moment, there is infinite possibility."
~ Victoria Moran

Respond to the following boxed sentence starters.

I am...

I hope...

I am great at...

I am grateful for...

I think I can...

I want to...

I hesitate...

I am excited to...

I believe that...

I enjoy...

I always...

Do You Multi-Task or Uni-Task?

If you're having an especially busy day and feeling overwhelmed by the amount of work to do, you may try taking a mindful approach. While many people pride themselves on the ability to do many things at once (multi-tasking), mindfulness experts suggest that we might want to do one task at a time (uni-task) to stay present in an activity. Some tips for uni-tasking include: minimize distractions, attend to one task alone, avoid outside distractions, clear your mind, turn off the cell phone and television, shut down social media and email, and work in short spurts.

Identify the times you have multi-tasked and explore ways that you can begin uni-tasking to actually accomplish more in a mindful way.

Example:
Project: Studying with a friend for a math test.
How I Multi-Tasked: I kept looking at my social media sites for updates.
Result: Neither of us did as well as we could have.
How I Could Have Uni-Tasked: I could have stopped worrying about social media and paid full attention to the material we were studying for the test and brainstorming with my friend.

Project:

How I Multi-Tasked:

Result:

How I Could Have Uni-Tasked:

Project:

How I Multi-Tasked:

Result:

How I Could Have Uni-Tasked:

Project:

How I Multi-Tasked:

Result:

How I Could Have Uni-Tasked:

"You can do two things at once, but you can't focus effectively on two things at once."
~ Gary Keller

Can You Slow Down, You Crazy Child?

Billy Joel sings, "Slow down, you crazy child. You're so ambitious for a juvenile."

Often, people are so anxious to begin the next task that they move too quickly through what they are presently doing, especially if they view it as a hassle. Rather than enjoying the task of creating something, people often hurry through the process to get to the finished product.

Using the first item as your template, doodle about those activities in which you move too fast, why you do so, and how you can slow down.

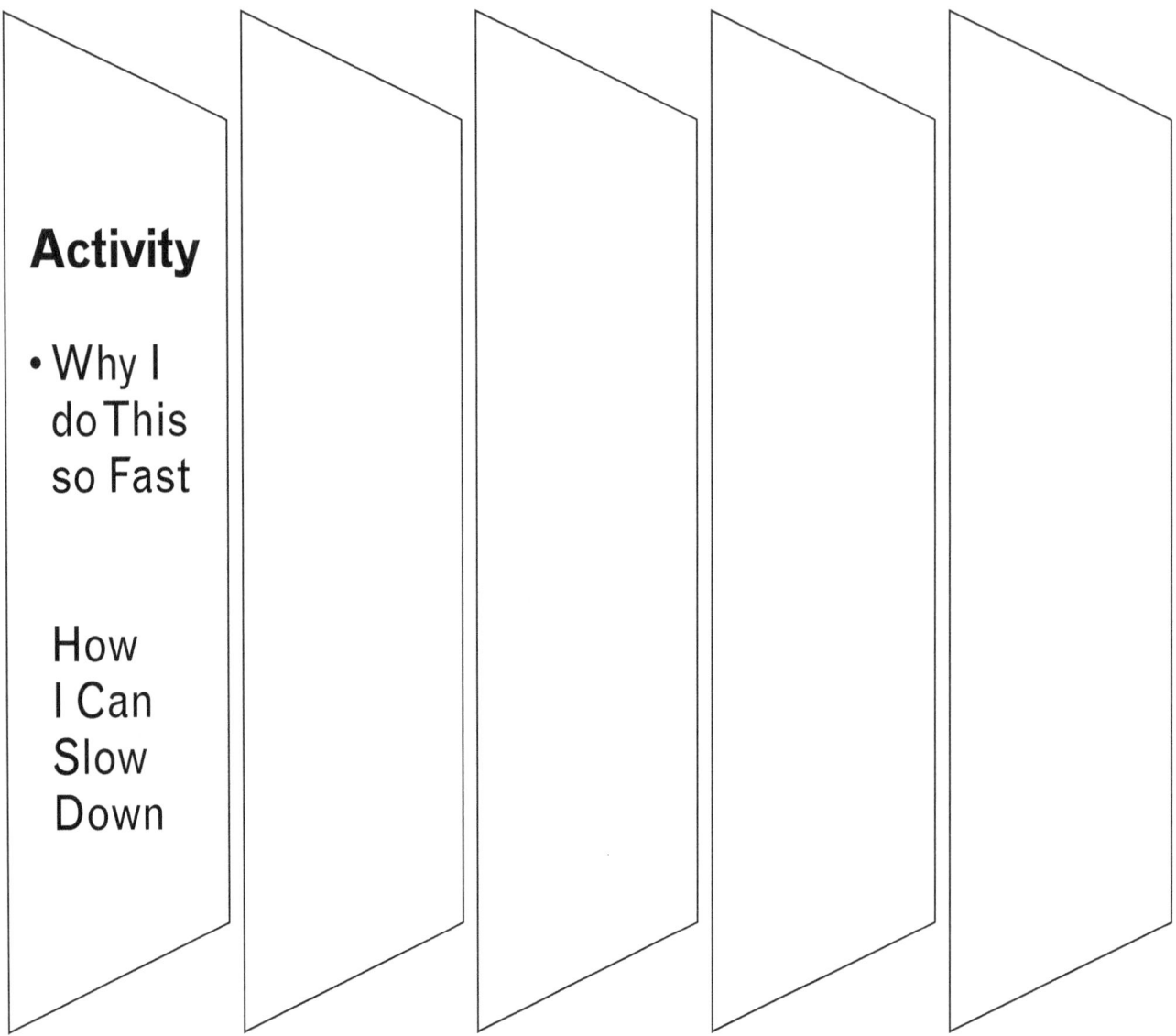

How can you become more mindful about all that you do?

_____
_____

Do You Think Too Much?

Sometimes people simply think too much! While they are supposedly doing something else, they are thinking about the writing project they need to finish, what to wear to school tomorrow, or what they want to do this weekend. They are not present in what they are doing, and thinking about too many other things won't allow them to fully appreciate what is happening right now.

What do you miss out on because you are thinking about other things?

One of the things I think too much about is…

Because of this, I miss…

The ways I can focus more are…

Another of the things I think too much about is…

Because of this, I miss…

The ways I can focus more are…

And another of the things I think too much about is…

Because of this, I miss…

The ways I can focus more are…

Are You Present When Listening?

When people are talking to each other, they often do not always give their full attention to being present by carefully listening. They may be thinking about something they must do, somewhere they must be, or what they want to say next to the person. It is important to focus your attention on fully listening without distraction or interruptions.

Some Tips for Listening Mindfully

Give others your full attention without letting your mind wander. You can do this by:
- Listen for the meaning behind the words of the other person. Think about the intentions that are beneath the words. What is the person really saying? What is the person really feeling?
- Maintain good eye contact without staring. Make eye contact, then, look away for a second. Repeat!
- Make an effort to find ways to remain present when speaking with others. Don't worry about your phone, others walking by, etc.
- Mindfully attend to what the person is saying verbally and nonverbally. Listen to the words and their underlying meaning, and then look to make sure their body language and words match each other.
- Mirror and reflect what you hear the other person saying. Say things like "You must have been frightened" or "I totally understand."
- Refrain from searching for a response while others are speaking. Listen fully, then, respond. Don't practice or rehearse what you will say next.
- Show interest and appropriate body language and tune out distractions to your conversation.

With one other person, have a conversation about what you did last weekend. First you speak and the other person listens, and then you each change roles. Each listener listens mindfully, using the tips above, and then each person answers the questions below:

How did it feel to listen mindfully? _____
_____
_____

How is it different from just listening? _____
_____
_____

How did it feel to have someone listen mindfully to you? _____
_____
_____

How is it that different from that person just listening? _____
_____
_____

Quotes about Being Present

In the spaces that follow, describe what each of the quotes mean to you and how each applies to your life.

"Life is available only in the present moment. If you abandon the present moment you cannot live the moments of your daily life deeply."
~ **Thich Nhat Hanh**

_____
_____
_____
_____
_____
_____
_____
_____

"The past, I think, has helped me appreciate the present—and I don't want to spoil any of it by fretting about the future."
~ **Audrey Hepburn**

_____
_____
_____
_____
_____
_____
_____
_____

CHAPTER 4

Do You Accept Others By Using Wise Judgment?

A BACKPACK OF MINDFULNESS TECHNIQUES

Throughout the "Do You Accept Others Using Wise Judgment?" chapter, you will find a variety of activity pages designed to help participants develop the ability to know when, and when not to, accept others by using wise judgment.

As your participants complete an activity in this chapter, you may want to refer to Chapter Five, "Do You Have a Backpack of Mindfulness Techniques?" for practical tools and techniques you can use to supplement and strengthen participant understanding of how to live a non-judgmental life, other than when judgments are necessary.

ACCEPTING OTHERS — Teen Mindfulness Skills Workbook

Practitioner's Discussion Prior to Each Handout

The suggested discussions are written for groups; however, you can easily adapt them when you are working with an individual.

Chapter 4 – Do You Accept Others Without Judging?

Do You Judge Others Wisely? 84
Explain to participants that while it is not always wise to be too judgmental, there are times when judging someone or something is a good thing! Ask someone to give an example.

Are You Aware of Your Judgmental Thoughts? 85
Ask participants what it means to be judgmental. After some discussion with examples, provide the following definition of judgmental: "Tending to judge people and situations too quickly and without reason."

How Accepting of Other People Are You? 86
Have a discussion about whether or not it is difficult to accept others for whom and for what they are. After the discussion, explain that when people can accept others as they are, they tend to be far less judgmental.

Do You Accept Situations for What They Are? 87
When people encounter daily hassles, they often judge the situation associated with the hassle using labels. Ask participants to brainstorm some of the labels that might be used to describe situations that are being judged.

Do You Sometimes Judge Too Fast? 88
Ask for volunteers to give an example of a time when they judged a situation too quickly.

What is an Opinionated Judgmental Person? 89
Ask for a volunteer to think of one of their opinions and present it to the group in a judgmental way, and then in a nonjudgmental way.

How Do You Judge Yourself? 90
Explain to the group that when you practice mindfulness, the goal is to let go of inappropriate judgment, including those one makes about oneself. *(Example: I am too heavy, I am not very smart, I am selfish, I am unworthy of love, etc.).* On the other hand, at times it IS mindful to judge yourself. *(Example: Is it safe? Will I be in danger?).* How are these situations different?

How Do You Negatively Judge Others? 91
Ask participants to name characteristics on which people are judged. To get them started, you might provide an example such as age or race. After people have completed the activity, ask for volunteers to share their own stories about being judged.

(Continued on the next page)

Practitioner's Discussion Prior to Each Handout *(Continued)*

Chapter 4 – Do You Accept Others Without Judging?

Are You Objective? 92
Explain the importance of objectively being aware of your environment. Ask for volunteers to name things in the room that they are noticing.

How Do You Show Empathy, Kindness, and Compassion? 93
Ask participants to explain the differences between empathy (being able to put yourself in the shoes of others to experience what they are experiencing), kindness (being friendly and generous), and compassion (sympathy and concern for the suffering and misfortunes of others).

How Do You Deal with Change? 94
Ask participants what is so scary about change? Ask for volunteers to tell about a change in their life that was scary and/or difficult for them. (Remind them, what's said in this group, stays in this group!)

Which Do You Do? 95
Ask someone to write "Overreacting" on the board. Provide the following definition: "Overreacting is to react to something too strongly or to respond to something with too powerful an emotion or with unnecessary or excessive action." Ask for volunteers to relay a situation in which someone overreacted. After each person tells a specific situation, ask for a show of hands if they believe it was an overreaction.

Do You Let Your Feelings Come and Go? 96
Tell participants that it is important to let feelings come and go without judging the situation. Ask for a volunteer to tell of a situation that was possible to let go without judging. Remind them not to name names.

How Are You Being Threatened? 97
Remind participants that when they react to a daily hassle as if it is a terrible, awful, harmful situation; it will prompt anxiety. Ask for a few volunteers to make up a story in which someone made a big deal out of nothing and then that person was extremely stressed afterwards.

What Daily Hassles Fill You With Worry, Anxiety & Stress? 98
Explain to participants that it is important to understand which daily hassles fill them with worry. This insight into their triggers can help to defuse some of the impact of these daily hassles. Ask for volunteers to state things they worry about in three words or less.

What is Happening When Someone is Mindful? 99
Explain that moment-to-moment awareness is learning to stop what you are doing, still your body, and observe what is going on in both body and mind, as well as around you. It is about cultivating intimacy with the present moment. When people experience moment-to-moment awareness, they are mindful of what is going on around them, as well as what is occurring within themselves. Ask participants: "If mindfulness would help you to rise above worry, anxiety, and stress, how would that change your life?

Do You Judge Others Wisely?

The ability to know when to judge wisely is a critical life skill. Think about some of the times you have judged others in the past, what criteria you used to make your judgments, and how it worked out. In each of the spaces on the left, draw or write about situations in which you judged others in a wise manner *(Example: I realized the person was an online predator. I told my parents, and I stopped using that site.)* **and in the right-hand column how you judged others in a not-so-wise manner** *(Example: I saw a friend passed out behind the school. I thought he was drunk. It turned out he was in a diabetic coma.)*

Wise Judgments I Have Made and Want to Keep Doing!

Not-So-Wise Judgments I Have Made and Want to Change!

Are You Aware of Your Judgmental Thoughts?

To be mindful, it is important to develop awareness of when you are being judgmental in an unfair way – not knowing the facts – or when you are judgmental in a fair way – knowing the facts and trusting your instincts. This means you need to be aware of your own thoughts and thought patterns, and, you need to be wise with your judgments.

Think about a situation in which you got caught up in a situation and wrongfully pre-judged the situation as well as wrongfully pre-judged the people involved, and acted in a way of which you were not proud. (Example: The person you just called fat has just lost 30 pounds; the girl you made fun of for crying had lost her father earlier that week; the person you kicked tells you he is also being abused at home.)

The situation: _____
_____
_____

The people involved: _____
_____
_____

Ways I judged them: _____
_____
_____

The thoughts that went through my head: _____
_____
_____

How could I have accepted the situation differently? _____
_____
_____

The next time you encounter a daily hassle, try these three steps with the people involved:

1) **Be Aware of any pre-conceived notions or stereotypes you have** – Try to monitor the thoughts going through your head. By doing this, you will be aware of the way your thoughts are attempting to judge the situation as good or bad, right or wrong, etc. This will reduce worry, anxiety, and stress.
2) **Develop understanding** – Try to understand the other person by being present and aware of the person's actions, speech patterns, and body language. Try to be empathetic and put yourself in the person's shoes. Think about what the person is trying to accomplish and how you can help.
3) **Accept, Accept, Accept** – Try to accept the situation for what it is without your thoughts interfering. Accept the person or people involved in the situation regardless of whether you agree or disagree with what is happening in the situation **unless it is dangerous, illegal, or just plain foolish.**

How Accepting of Other People Are You?

When people encounter daily hassles, they often tend to judge the people associated with the hassle. Mindful people accept others the way they are. They understand that a person's behavior is, for the most part, not for them to judge, unless they are given a good reason to judge that person in a negative way. *(Example: illegal, dangerous, foolish, etc.)*. When people can accept others as they are, they tend to be far less judgmental. Think about the daily hassles in your life and the people associated with them.

Identify THREE PEOPLE who are in some way involved in your annoying hassles, if and how you judge them, and if you feel you can accept them as they are, or not.

My Daily Hassle with Person # 1: _____
_____

The person involved: _____
_____

Ways I judge this person: _____
_____

How can I accept this person as is? _____
_____

If I can't accept this person as is, why can't I? _____
_____

My Daily Hassle with Person # 2: _____
_____

The person involved: _____
_____

Ways I judge this person: _____
_____

How can I accept this person as is? _____
_____

If I can't accept this person as is, why can't I? _____
_____

My Daily Hassle with Person # 3: _____
_____

The person involved: _____
_____

Ways I judge this person: _____
_____

How can I accept this person as is: _____
_____

If I can't accept this person as is, why can't I? _____
_____

Do You Accept Situations for What They Are?

When people encounter daily hassles, they tend to judge the situation associated with the hassle using such labels as wonderful, catastrophic, horrible, etc. Mindful people accept situations for the way they naturally are. They do not attempt to attach labels to, or change, these situations. They understand that a situation is, for the most part, not for them to judge, unless they are given a good reason to judge that situation in a positive or negative way. It is important to look at and evaluate the situations involved in daily hassles just as they are.

Identify three of your daily hassles, the situation itself, the labels you attach to the situation, and if and how you can be more accepting of the situation.

The Daily Hassle # 1: _____

The first situation involved: _____

The labels I attach to this situation: _____

How can I accept this situation as is? _____

If I can't accept this situation as is, why can't I? _____

My Daily Hassle # 2: _____

The second situation involved: _____

The labels I attach to this situation: _____

How can I accept this situation as is? _____

If I can't accept this situation as is, why can't I? _____

My Daily Hassle # 3: _____

The third situation involved: _____

The labels I attach to this situation: _____

How can I accept this situation as is? _____

If I can't accept this situation as is, why can't I? _____

Do You Sometimes Judge Too Fast?

We often have experiences which we tend to judge quickly and subconsciously, and then we can lose out. Our minds tend to respond automatically, often triggered by negative, unwise, or irrational thinking. By being mindful, people are able to focus their attention in the present, observe what goes on around them without associating judgment to it, decide if they are being fair or not fair, and recognize when wise judgment needs to come into play.

Fill in the table below and identify your judgments.

Experiences I Tend to Judge	My Feelings Associated With Each Judgment	Is this Fair or NOT Fair?
Example: When a new student comes to our school I am unlikely to invite the person into our group because of the differences between us.	*I am reluctant to give myself a chance to get to know the person, or give that person a chance to get to know me because I am wary of the perceived differences.*	☐ Fair ☑ Not Fair
		☐ Fair ☐ Not Fair
		☐ Fair ☐ Not Fair
		☐ Fair ☐ Not Fair
		☐ Fair ☐ Not Fair
		☐ Fair ☐ Not Fair
		☐ Fair ☐ Not Fair

What is an Opinionated, Judgmental Person?

Rather than judging your thoughts and experiences as good or bad, right or wrong, hurtful or helpful, smart or stupid, it is best to simply observe them with compassionate non-attachment. An opinionated, judgmental person can be described as someone who rushes to negative judgments without a good reason. It can describe someone who forms lots of opinions, often harsh or critical, about other people or themselves. This type of person is not very open-minded, easygoing, or compassionate. They usually assign a label to someone or something as good or as bad. This type of judgmental person will react based on negative thoughts, emotions, and opinions.

Some examples of judgmental thoughts about others and self:

"I'm feeling lonely. Nobody likes me."
"My friend hasn't texted me. She must be angry."
"My friend won't go to the movie with me. I hate her."
"My teacher never calls on me in class. He must not like me."
"That person in my English class has dirty clothes. She must be poor."
"That waiter hardly spoke to me. He is really rude. I'm going to complain to his manager."

Another Way to Look at it!
Change your words. Change your mindset,

In these types of situations, the brain is assigning labels so quickly to the situation that the experiences are tainted before they can be thought out and processed. Mindfulness, on the other hand, is about being aware of our brain's tendency to do this and slowing down enough to take a fresh, open perspective in a detached manner. Look at the examples again, and write about what a person who is NOT judgmental might think.

Example: "I'm feeling lonely. ~~Nobody likes me.~~"
My friends might be busy. I will make some calls.

"I'm feeling lonely. ~~Nobody likes me.~~"
_____

"My friend hasn't texted me. ~~She must be angry.~~"
_____

"That waiter didn't speak to me. ~~He is really rude. I'm going to complain to his manager.~~"
_____

"My teacher never calls on me in class. ~~He must not like me.~~"
_____

"My friend won't go to the movie with me. ~~I hate her.~~"
_____

"That person in my English class has dirty clothes. ~~She must be poor.~~"
_____

How Do You Judge Yourself?

We tend to judge things all day, every day, including ourselves. This process can often create worry, anxiety, and stress. We judge things we like or don't like; things that irritate us; things that do not make sense to us; things that we love or don't love; and how successful or not we are. When you practice mindfulness, the goal is to let go of inappropriate judgment, including those we make about ourselves. *(Example: heavy, smart, selfish, unworthy, unreliable, thrifty, etc.).* **However, at times it IS mindful to judge yourself.** *(Example: Will I have the willpower to say no to drugs and alchol at a friends party?)*

What types of judgments do you make about yourself?

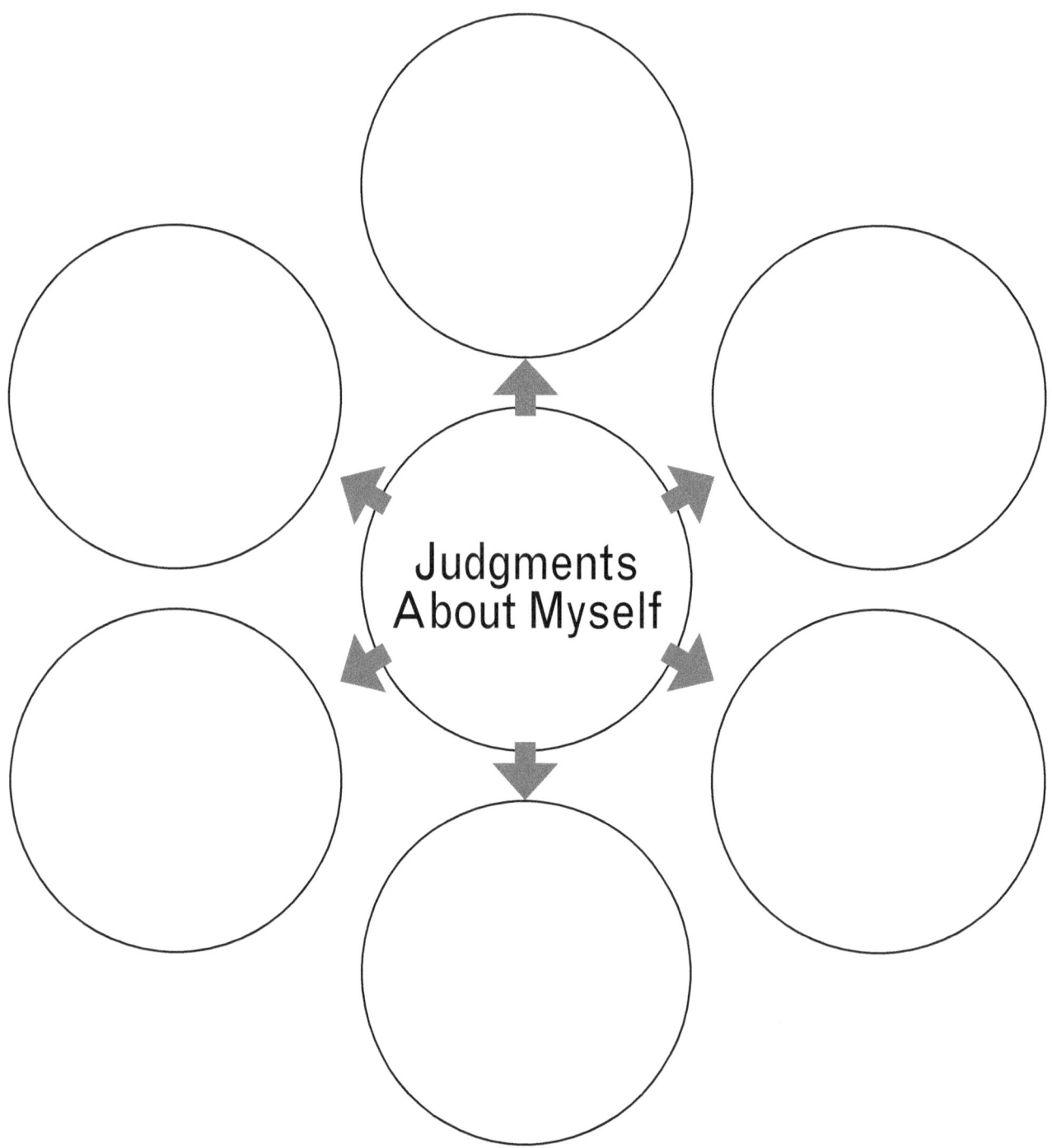

How Do You Negatively Judge Others?

In your interactions with others, are you aware of how you judge them? Think about your interactions, and how you judge the actions and words of others, right or wrong, or what it is they are saying or not saying. Think about some of the times you have judged people based on personal characteristics.

Complete the table below to explore how you might be judging others. Use NAME CODES.

The Ways I Negatively Judge Others	How I React or Show This Negative Judgment (Use a name code)	The Effect This Judgment Has on Me, On the Person, and/or On Our Relationship
Example: Possessions	I am envious of SWW's clothes, shoes, and dyed hair. I feel like a mess when I am around her. I don't want to go anywhere with her because people will compare us.	She is upset because I won't go places with her. I feel jealous and I know I am losing her as a friend. She thinks she did something wrong.
Lifestyle	He is into drugs and I have made it clear to him that I want no part of it and will not go anywhere with him.	He is not willing to give up drugs. Our friendship is pretty much over as I don't trust him and won't go anywhere with him.
Possessions		
School		
Lifestyle		
Physical Appearance		
Age or Gender		
Race, Culture, Nationality		
Safe or Unsafe Choices		
Treatment of Others		
Other		

Are You Objective?

Mindful people are constantly aware of their environment. They notice the way things look; how things have changed; the colors, textures, beauty; upkeep, not cared for, etc.

For this activity, observe your current surroundings, and be objective. Don't judge anything, just describe in the spaces below.

Example: My Surroundings: My back yard
The grass is bright green.   There are weeds in the grass.   The daffodils are in bloom.
The bird house has a bird in it with eggs!   The bird bath has no water in it.   It is hot outside.

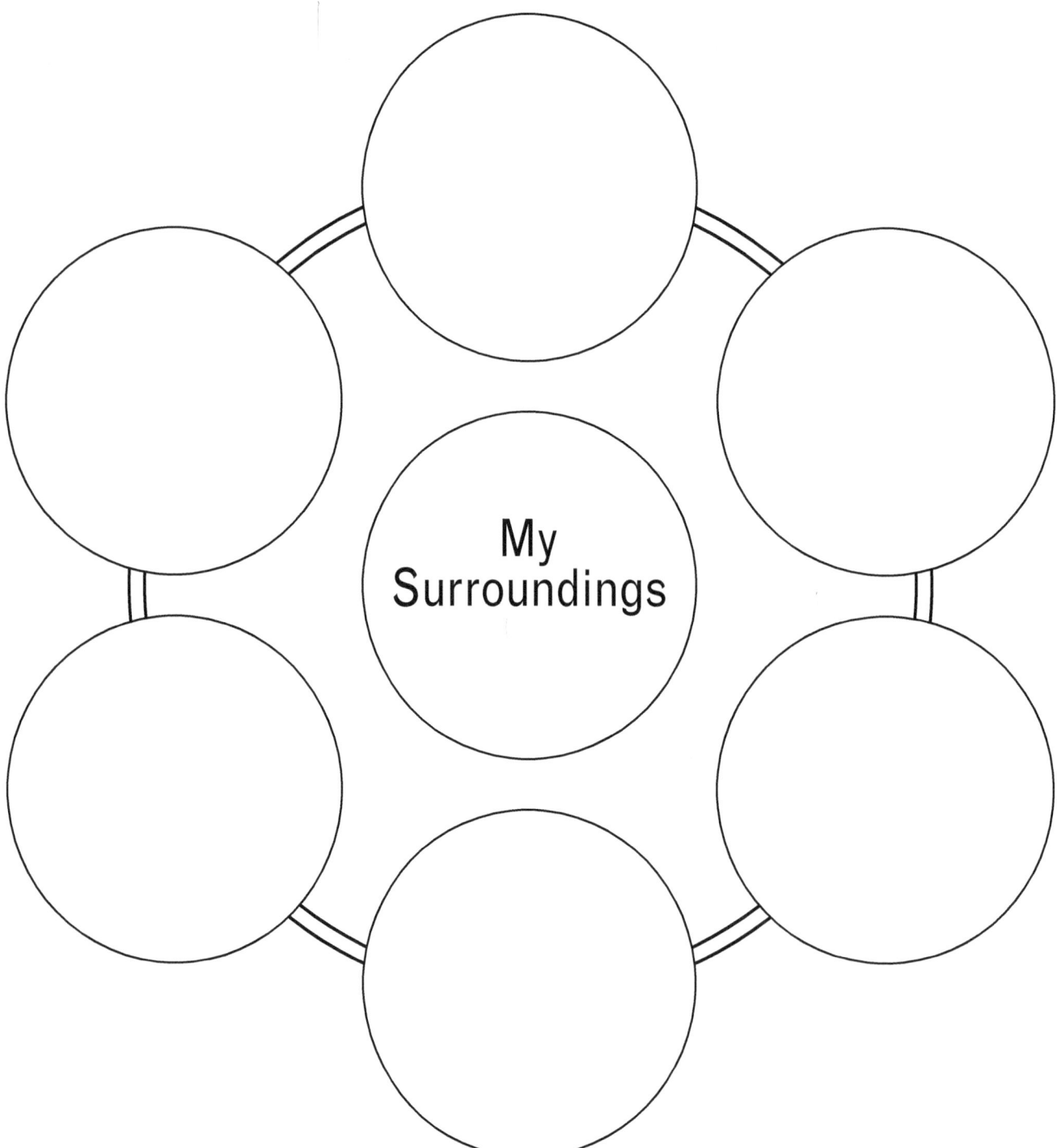

How Do You Show Empathy, Kindness, and Compassion?

Mindful people are not so detached that they take others for granted. Actually, the opposite is true. They are usually present for whatever occurs. Mindfulness requires being in the present without judgment, but this does not suggest that mindful people detach so much that they do not show empathy, kindness, and compassion for other people.

Look at the following example, and then answer the questions that follow.

> **You are planning to go to the movies with your friends. Someone in your class is having trouble with math and has an exam coming up in the morning. He asks if you would come over and tutor him.**

What would be a negative reaction someone might have to this situation?
_____
_____

Why might someone experience a negative reaction?
_____
_____

What judgments might contribute to a negative reaction?
_____
_____

How could someone suspend judgment in this situation?
_____
_____

How well do we need to know someone to be able to suspend judgment in this situation?
_____
_____

It is important to treat others with kindness and compassion. What would be a kind and compassionate reaction?
_____
_____

How might a person feel for showing kindness and compassion?
_____
_____

How might a person feel for having been shown kindness and compassion?
_____
_____

How Do You Deal with Change?

Change can often bring worry, anxiety, and stress. Accepting hassles as they are, and knowing what you can change and what you cannot change, is one of the core principles in being a mindful person. Mindful people are able to accept each moment as it is without judging it. They consider whether a change is really needed or not. They know that they can change themselves and also know that they cannot change another person.

Explore some of the situations that cause you to worry, feel anxious, and/or be stressed out. Then, explore the things you can change about these situations and the things you cannot. Finally, explore ways that you can be more accepting of the things you cannot change.

Situation	Worry, Anxiety, or Stress	What I Can Change	What I Can Accept
Example: My step-mom has been sick for a few weeks.	*I am extremely worried about her, anxious when the phone rings, and stressed out by thinking about it all of the time.*	*I help as much as I can to make it easier on her but I can't change her health, and I still need to go to school.*	*I will resume my social life when she gets better. I have explained it to my friends and they understand.*

"Grant me the serenity
to accept the things I cannot change;
courage to change the things I can;
and wisdom to know the difference."
~ Reinhold Niebuhr

Which Do You Do?

It is important to learn to consciously react from a non-judgmental perspective. When you are able to do this and stop overreacting you will be on your way to being mindful. The following exercise is designed to help you compare and contrast a reactive and a detached perspective to a daily hassle. Think about this situation:

> You are driving along and all of a sudden, another car swerves in front of you and cuts you off. The other car almost hits your car.

In the box that follows, draw or describe how you might react if you decide that the other driver is a real jerk.

In the box that follows, draw or describe how you might react if you decide that it all came out okay.

What are the ways you believe you would have reacted? Explain.

_____

_____

_____

Do You Let Your Feelings Come and Go?

A goal of mindfulness involves being in the present, even during daily hassles, and letting go of judgments, fears, regrets, and expectations. The problem is that all people experience both positive and negative emotions. The secret is to embrace your emotions, then allow them to pass like clouds in the sky. You can't control clouds, but you can let them pass. The same is true about your emotions.

In each of the clouds, describe a daily hassle and the positive or negative emotions associated with it. Then imagine that it simply floats away. This will reduce your levels of worry, stress, and anxiety.

Example: The school bus is late in coming to pick you up. This will make you late for school. Your emotions might be anger, frustration, and impatience.

How Are You Being Threatened?

Many people react to daily hassles as if they are harmful situations that prompt worry, anxiety, and stress. By focusing on staying in the present moment, it becomes easier not to judge others, as judgment tends to come from a potential threat or prediction of how one's behavior will affect the future.

Explore your daily hassles, the judgments you associate with these hassles, and the perceived threat that triggers strong emotions.

Daily Hassles	How I Judge It	Perceived Threat
Example: I have tons of homework in my algebra class.	When will I ever use algebra anyway?	I am neglecting my grades in this class and it might spoil my GPA.

Which of the situations above can you view in a non-judgmental manner? _____
_____
_____

If not, how can you successfully change the situation? _____
_____
_____

What Daily Hassles Fill You With Worry, Anxiety & Stress?

Daily hassles happen to everyone and can fill you with worry, anxiety, and stress. They can be viewed from a positive, detached, non-judgmental perspective. This is an important mindfulness technique.

Draw or doodle how you will handle the sentence starters below. Have fun!

My daily hassles are...	How can I view situations without judging them in the future?
Ways I typically react are...	**How can I react in a non-judgmental way?**

What is Happening When Someone is Mindful?

When people experience moment-to-moment awareness, they are mindful of what is going on around them, as well as what is occurring within themselves. They rise above worry, anxiety, and stress. This is a critical component of developing mindfulness. It includes learning to stop what you are doing, still your body, and observe what is going on in both body and mind, as well as around you. It is about cultivating intimacy with the present moment.

Write one of your daily hassles in the center circle and allow yourself to feel the worry, anxiety, or stress that you would usually experience. Write those feelings next to each circle.

Quotes about Non-Judgmental Awareness

In the spaces that follow, describe what each of the quotes mean to you and how each quote applies to your life.

"Mindfulness means moment-to-moment, non-judgmental awareness. It is cultivated by refining our capacity to pay attention, intentionally, in the present moment, and then sustaining that attention over time as best we can. In the process, we become more in touch with our life as it is unfolding."
~ Jon Kabat-Zinn

_____

_____

_____

_____

_____

_____

_____

"Mindfulness is the aware, balanced acceptance of the present experience. It isn't more complicated than that. It is opening to or receiving the present moment, pleasant or unpleasant, just as it is, without either clinging to it or rejecting it."
~Sylvia Boorstein

_____

_____

_____

_____

_____

_____

_____

CHAPTER 5

Do You Have a Backpack of Mindfulness Techniques?

A BACKPACK OF MINDFULNESS TECHNIQUES

To supplement the variety of activities in the first four chapters of this workbook, this chapter provides an additional collection of powerful, mindfulness exercises as well as easy-to-understand practices that can be used to develop moment-by-moment awareness in any situation and at any time when living a mindful life.

Practitioner's Discussion Prior to Each Handout

The suggested discussions are written for groups; however, you can easily adapt them when you are working with an individual.

Chapter 5 – Do You Have a Backpack of Mindfulness Techniques?

How Mindful Are You? 108
Ask volunteers to describe ways they are mindful, and ways they are not mindful.

Do You Tune In to Your Sensations? 109
Explain to participants that people who are mindful are attentive to the sensations that are occurring in their bodies, both during times of stress and non-stress. Ask volunteers for their own examples.

Can You Sense Your Senses? 111
Ask participants to identify which sense they are most mindful with, and ask them to give an example: sound, sight, smell, taste, or touch.

How Can You Start Your Day Mindfully? 112
Explain to participants that a great beginning of your day is to start it off mindfully. Ask participants to brainstorm ways they can be more mindful at the beginning of the day.

How Can You Reframe, then Detach, from Your Thoughts? 113
Reframing is putting a realistic and positive spin on your thoughts. Ask for volunteers to put a positive spin on this first thought of the morning. "It's going to be a crummy day today. It's pouring!"

How Can You Activate Your Senses? 114
Ask participants to jot down their observations of the environment around them. Then, ask them to pair up and compare their responses. Ask the pairs what they learned from and about each other.

Can You Meditate While Walking? YES! 115
Ask for a show of hands of people who meditate. Ask if there are volunteers who will explain how and when they meditate. *(Example: the shower, in line at the store, walking, etc.)*

Can You Meditate While Concentrating on the Outdoors? YES! 116
Talk about the fact that the outdoors and nature can be a great place to meditate and to be mindful of one's environment. Ask participants to share how they usually feel when they are outdoors.

What are Good Reasons to Meditate? 117
Explain that different people have different reasons for meditating. Ask for volunteers to each state one of those reasons.

(Continued on the next page)

| Teen Mindfulness Skills Workbook — **MINDFULNESS TECHNIQUES**

Practitioner's Discussion
Prior to Each Handout *(Continued)*

Chapter 5 – Do You Have a Backpack of Mindfulness Techniques?

Where Can You Meditate? 118
　Explain that different people enjoy meditating in different ways, times, and places. Ask volunteers to share how, when, and where they meditate.

How Can You Observe in a Mindful Way? 119
　Ask for volunteers to pick an object that they have with them and, without looking at it, describe it. *(Example: wallet, purse, shoes, cell phone, pen, etc.)* Then, ask them to display the object and see how observant they were.

Have You Tried Mindfulness Meditation? 120
　Provide this definition of mindfulness meditation: "Mindfulness mediation is the act of meditating, clearing your mind of any thoughts, dismissing any thoughts that pop into your head, and while doing this, trying to be mindful of sensation, noises, etc." Ask them how easy or difficult it was.

Can You Journal About Mindfulness? 121
　Ask for a show of hands of people who journal. Discuss the value of journaling.

Does Mindfulness Bring Awareness? 122
　Remind participants that it is important to maintain mindfulness in everyday activities. Ask for volunteers to state which activity they would like to do more mindfully.

Do You Eat Mindfully? 123
　Write the words "MINDFUL EATING" on the board. Ask participants to describe some of the problems that might be associated with not eating mindfully. Examples might include eating too much, eating too fast, not appreciating the tastes and aromas, etc.

Can You Bring Awareness to Your Breath? 124
　Ask for a show of hands of people who use deep breathing to relax.
　Ask for a few volunteers to demonstrate how they do it.

What is Abdominal Breathing? 125
　Ask people if they are ever aware of their breathing. Distribute the handouts, and provide participants with time to practice the activity. Then, ask participants to discuss their experiences.

(Continued on the next page)

Practitioner's Discussion Prior to Each Handout *(Continued)*

Chapter 5 – Do You Have a Backpack of Mindfulness Techniques?

Have You Tried Breathing to Avoid Being Judgmental? 126
  Ask participants: "How can you possibly turn off the automatic-judgment machine that lives in your head?" Assure them by counting breaths, they will be able to do it. Refer to the handout.

How Can You Practice Mindfulness Appreciation? 127
  Tell participants that it is critical to be mindfully appreciative of the people in their lives. Ask participants to identify one person in their life whom they appreciate, and discuss why they appreciate that person. They do not need to name the person.

Can You Maintain Your Focus? 129
  Describe the importance of maintaining focus. You may need to read this to them a few times: "Sit with your posture straight; choose an object you would like to concentrate on; relax and focus your attention on it as long as you can. Try not to let your gaze wander, and if it does, return your focus. Do not judge or think about the object in any way, simply observe it. Appreciate the qualities of the object." After a few minutes recall them to the group. Ask them how this process felt.

How Can You Be More Aware of Your Body? 130
  Ask participants: "How does your body feel when you are feeling worried, anxious, or stressed?"

Are You Thinking Again? 131
  Explain that we often think things without even being aware that we are doing so. This can be a problem for many people. Thoughts and judgments are generated automatically and can interfere with one's awareness and concentration, keeping one from being in the present. Ask for volunteers to explain how, when, and where their mind just keeps on thinking, even when they don't want it to.

Can You Be Thankful? 132
  Describe the importance of being introspective and developing a state of mindfulness. People often forget to be thankful for the everyday wonderments in our life. Ask volunteers to share when and how they can begin to spend time sitting quietly.

How Mindful Are You?

As the pace of life continues to increase, and teens are busier than they have ever been, mindfulness becomes an antidote to the stress of daily hassles. It is important to explore how mindful you are in your daily life.

On the line of each of the seven characteristics of mindfulness listed below, place an X on the continuum of how mindful you are. Write on the line below why you rated yourself in that particular way.

I usually focus on the present moment, not the past or the future.

0 (Not Like Me) • 5 (Somewhat Like Me) • 10 (Much Like Me)

....

I am aware of what my body tells me.

0 (Not Like Me) • 5 (Somewhat Like Me) • 10 (Much Like Me)

....

I am able to manage my worry, anxiety, and/or stress.

0 (Not Like Me) • 5 (Somewhat Like Me) • 10 (Much Like Me)

....

I am non-judgmental about people.

0 (Not Like Me) • 5 (Somewhat Like Me) • 10 (Much Like Me)

....

I accept most things as they are.

0 (Not Like Me) • 5 (Somewhat Like Me) • 10 (Much Like Me)

....

I am not overly attached to most situations.

0 (Not Like Me) • 5 (Somewhat Like Me) • 10 (Much Like Me)

....

I am kind and compassionate.

0 (Not Like Me) • 5 (Somewhat Like Me) • 10 (Much Like Me)

Do You Tune in to Your Sensations?

Mindful teens are attentive to the sensations that are occurring in their bodies, both during times of stress and non-stress. These sensations can alert you to the stress that might be occurring in your life. It is important to practice mindfulness by tuning in to your body. Start slowly, and soon it will be a habit. Review each of the following situations and describe how you tune into your bodily sensations.

After you send an email or text, notice how your body feels. What muscles are activated, what parts of your body are most affected? Are you hot, cold, or neutral in temperature? What's your posture like?

How does this reflect the message you just sent? _____
_____
_____

You are watching a controversial politician or celebrity speak. Which muscles are activated, what parts of your body are most affected? Are you hot, cold, or neutral in temperature? What's your posture like?

How does this reflect what you are watching? _____
_____
_____

You have just been asked to do something you hate to do. What muscles are activated, what parts of your body are most affected? Are you hot, cold, or neutral in temperature? What's your posture like?

How does this reflect how you will engage in the task? _____
_____
_____

You are walking down the hallway and you see someone being bullied by several people. What muscles are activated, what parts of your body are most affected? Are you hot, cold, or neutral in temperature? What's your posture like?

How does this reflect the way you will engage the situation? _____
_____
_____

(Continued on the next page)

Do You Tune in to Your Sensations? *(Continued)*

Teens experience worry, anxiety, and stress for a variety of reasons. Regardless of why or what situations may trigger these feelings in you, you can easily reduce their effect on you by using progressive muscle relaxation. When you worry, become anxious, and/or feel stress in your body try this progressive muscle relaxation technique:

- Focus on your breathing. Slow, even, regular breaths. Breathe in relaxation and breathe out tension… in relaxation, and out tension. Continue to breathe slowly and rhythmically.
- Now, still breathing slowly, start with your toes. Relax and let all of the tension go from your toes. Feel the muscles going limp, loose, and relaxed. Notice how relaxed the muscles feel now. Feel the difference between tension and relaxation. Now do the same with your feet, ankles, and calves, keeping them all relaxed. Continue onto your thighs and then your buttocks.
- Work your way up to your stomach, chest, arms, hands, and fingers, shoulders, neck, mouth, eye lids, and the top of your head.
- Notice all of the muscles in your body. Notice how relaxed your muscles feel.
- Allow any last bits of tension to drain away.
- Enjoy the relaxation you are experiencing.
- Notice your calm breathing. Enjoy the relaxation for a few moments.
- When you are ready to return to your usual level of alertness and awareness, slowly begin to re-awaken your body.
- Wiggle your toes and fingers. Swing your arms gently. Shrug your shoulders. Stretch if you like.

This progressive muscle relaxation technique will leave you feeling calm and refreshed.

Journal about how you felt WHILE using this technique.

_____
_____
_____
_____

Journal about how you felt AFTER using this technique.

_____
_____
_____
_____

Can You Sense Your Senses?

During the worry, anxiety, and stress of the daily hassles in your life, one helpful mindfulness practice is to tune into your own senses. It sounds easy, but it takes some practice. It is important to start small and work up to reducing your reactions to your daily hassles.

As you do each of these actions, notice and describe your sensory experiences.

*As you eat your lunch, notice how it **tastes** and **smells**, the sound of chewing, etc.*

*When you wash your hands, notice the temperature of the water and how it **feels** on your skin.*

*When you were driving or riding in a vehicle, what did you **notice** or **hear**?*

*When you were driving or riding in a vehicle, what did you **feel**?*

Describe one of your everyday hassles that happened this day — large or small.

When this hassle occurred, what did your senses tell you?

When this hassle occurred, what did you particularly notice?

When this hassle occurred, what thoughts were going through your head?

How Can You Start Your Day Mindfully?

A great beginning of your day is to start it off mindfully, thus reducing any worry, anxiety, and/ or stress associated with your day. Practice this exercise for five minutes at the start of each day for one week.

As you awaken in the morning, lie still with your eyes closed, breathe in, and pay attention to how it feels to hold in your breath. As you exhale slowly, imagine sunlight enveloping your body and bathing you in bright, warm light. Hold this image for a few minutes and focus on it. Then open your eyes, rise slowly, and say,

"I will stay in the light throughout the day."

Each day, journal your reactions, how you felt, and its impact on the rest of the day.

Day 1	
Day 2	
Day 3	
Day 4	
Day 5	
Day 6	
Day 7	

What phrase(s), other than *"I will stay in the light throughout the day."* would you like to try?

_____

_____

How Can You Reframe, then Detach, from Your Thoughts?

One of the secrets about mindfulness is to avoid becoming involved in negative thoughts as they arise during the worry, anxiety, and/or stress of your daily hassles. Reframing, or putting a realistic and positive spin on your thoughts can help you to more easily accept then dismiss them. It is important to be aware of and accept your negative thinking, then reframe your thoughts so you can stay detached and not allow negative thoughts to affect you adversely.

Below, explore some of your daily hassles. After you have identified these stressful hassles, journal about your thoughts related to them. Next, reframe the negative thoughts so that they are less harmful to you and allow you to detach more easily.

My Daily Hassle	My Thoughts	How I Can Reframe The Thought(s)
Example: I need to take my younger brother to school with me and back home.	*My friends think I'm weird for doing this!*	*It gives me time with my brother. I don't care what others think.*

How Can You Activate Your Senses?

Often people go through life unaware of all the sights, sounds, tastes, smells, and touches around them. Even though their eyes are open, they do not see the wonders of the world in which we live.

Spend a day tuned into your senses while you're walking. During that day, jot down all of your observations of the world around you.

Sights	Sounds	Tastes	Smells	Touch

Can You Meditate While Walking? YES!

One way to develop mindfulness is with the everyday practice of walking. The exciting thing about this meditation is that you can do it at any time and any where you are walking. When you are feeling the effects of stress, or encountering a daily hassle, you can take a few minutes and go for a walk.

Practice meditative walking by concentrating on every step you take.

At first do this when taking just 10 steps. Describe how it felt and why. _____
_____
_____
_____

Practice walking by connecting each of your steps to various parts of your body and its movements. How did this help you to stay present by observing your body's movements? _____
_____
_____
_____

Think about how your muscles are activated throughout each step.
How did this help you to stay present by thinking about and noticing your muscles? _____
_____
_____
_____

Now try doing this for several hundred feet, while maintaining your concentration on which ever process works well for you. How did this feel? _____
_____
_____
_____

How did this help you to stay present by your various observations? _____
_____
_____
_____

Which of the observations—concentrating on the steps, noticing the body movements, or noticing your muscles in action—worked best for you, and why? _____
_____
_____
_____

Can You Meditate While Concentrating on the Outdoors? YES!

Develop mindfulness with the everyday practice of walking and noticing everything around you.

Take a walk outside and when you come in, write down what you noticed.

The colors and the sizes of the trees and bushes. _____
_____
_____
_____

Are there flowers blooming? What kind? What color? _____
_____
_____
_____

Were there birds? What were the sounds of their chirping? What kind? What color? _____
_____
_____
_____

Did you walk on sidewalks? Were there cracks in them? _____
_____
_____
_____

Did you see or hear traffic? What were the sounds? _____
_____
_____
_____

Did you see or hear other people? Did you acknowledge them? Did they acknowledge you?
_____
_____
_____

What else did you notice? _____
_____
_____
_____

What are Good Reasons to Meditate?

Different people have different reasons to meditate. Check those that might be possibilities for you, even if it's a mini-meditation. Next to it, write why it might or does work for you.

☐ Are able to discontinue addictive habits _____

☐ Avoid burnout _____

☐ Be kinder to others _____

☐ Become less frustrated _____

☐ Bring out own creativity _____

☐ Cut down on pain-killers _____

☐ Demonstrate congeniality with others _____

☐ De-stress _____

☐ Display good work ethics _____

☐ Enjoy better physical health _____

☐ Exercise patience when waiting _____

☐ Exhibit less intense reactions _____

☐ Feel more content _____

☐ Focus on healthy eating _____

☐ Function with good mental health _____

☐ Gain from a greater awareness _____

☐ Have patience _____

☐ Improve study habits _____

☐ Increase acceptance _____

☐ Keep a positive attitude _____

☐ Let go of worries _____

☐ Nurture a close relationship _____

☐ Obtain higher grades _____

☐ Receive good reviews from boss _____

☐ Relieve anxiety _____

☐ Retain a calm demeanor _____

☐ Show a relaxed approach _____

☐ Sleep peacefully _____

☐ Stand up to an abuser _____

☐ Stop abuse _____

☐ Tone down one's temper _____

☐ Other _____

☐ Other _____

Where Can You Meditate?

Different people find different places to meditate. Check those that might be possibilities for you, even if it's a mini-meditation. Next to it, write why it might or does work for you.

☐ Bath tub or shower _____

☐ Beach _____

☐ Bed _____

☐ Bus, plane, or train _____

☐ Concert _____

☐ Doctor's or Dentist's office _____

☐ Gym _____

☐ House of worship _____

☐ Mountains _____

☐ Ocean _____

☐ Open field _____

☐ Outdoor park _____

☐ Parked car _____

☐ Peaceful setting _____

☐ Pool _____

☐ Quiet place in the house _____

☐ Recliner or rocking chair _____

☐ River _____

☐ Rock concert _____

☐ School during a break _____

☐ Sunrise _____

☐ Sunset _____

☐ Swing set _____

☐ Almost anywhere! _____

How Can You Observe in a Mindful Way?

Take an everyday object, like your phone, water bottle, or pen. For sixty seconds, look at it, feel it, and observe it, without passing judgment about it. Just observe it for what it actually is. Then describe (or draw it) below.

What did you observe about this object that you had never noticed before?

_____

_____

_____

Have You Tried Mindful Meditation?

Mindful meditation is a great way to train your brain to live in the present moment without placing a judgment on it. By doing this, people are able to notice their thoughts and simply note them and watch as they float away or dissolve. Mindful meditation takes time and practice, but is very worthwhile! It will help you be more present in your everyday life and allow you to let go or manage some of those everyday hassles.

Start Now

- Find a quiet spot and make sure you are comfortable, but not comfortable enough to fall asleep. You can sit in a chair if you prefer or on a cushion on the floor.
- Close your eyes and concentrate on your breathing.
- Thoughts will pop into your head and attempt to distract your concentration on your breathing.
- Try not to get distracted by your thoughts, simply notice them and let them pass by.
- What do you hear?
- What do you smell?
- What do you sense?
- Pay attention to how you feel while doing this. How do you feel physically? Emotionally?

After you have done the above mindful meditation for five minutes, describe or draw the experience below:

Can You Journal About Mindfulness?

Mindfulness is about paying attention to what you are doing in the present moment and being willing to bring your mind back to focus in a gentle manner. Different people practice mindfulness during everyday activities in different ways. *(Examples: Upon waking up, outdoor in nature letting one's mind wander, during a concert, cleaning one's room, working on a project, exercising, waiting for a doctor appointment, etc.)*

Start keeping a journal about those times when you were, or are, mindful. Journaling will help you to explore the unique characteristics of your mindful moments. To get started, write about a time when you experienced mindfulness. Use the following questions to structure your journaling entry.

Where you were and what you were doing?
How you were able to focus your mind?
On what did you focus?
What you were aware of?

How did it feel during that time?
And how did it feel afterwards?
What was occurring with your breathing?
How did you keep refocusing your attention?

_____
_____
_____
_____
_____
_____
_____
_____
_____
_____
_____
_____
_____
_____
_____
_____
_____
_____
_____
_____

Does Mindfulness Bring Awareness?

It is important to maintain mindfulness in your everyday activities. This sounds easy, but it takes practice.

Choose one routine activity that you do everyday like showering, doing homework, listening to music, etc. For the next week, try and do this activity mindfully, and journal about your results. Bring awareness to every step of the activity.

Days of the Week	My Awareness Journal
Sunday	
Monday	
Tuesday	
Wednesday	
Thursday	
Friday	
Saturday	

What did you notice throughout the week? _____

_____

_____

Do You Eat Mindfully?

Many people rush through their meals, often not being able to remember what they ate. Many people eat in front of a television or a computer. Many people eat out with friends and are so busy talking that they don't pay attention to the food. When people eat these various ways they may lose track of the sensation and taste of food. This can lead to overeating, not eating enough, eating too fast, and not being concerned about healthy foods.

The next time you eat, try being more mindful using these techniques:

Do not attempt to engage in other activities when you eat. Just eat. How did that feel?

_____

_____

_____

At home, sit at a table. How did that feel?

_____

_____

_____

How did the food look? Smell?

_____

_____

_____

Eat slowly. This will make food more satisfying to you and make you less likely to crave additional snacks. How did that feel?

_____

_____

_____

Pay attention to every bite. How did every bite taste?

_____

_____

_____

Can You Bring Your Awareness to Your Breath?

As most people experience daily hassles and stressors, they notice that their natural breathing becomes shallow and labored.

Five Steps in Bringing Awareness to Your Breathing

Step One
- Relax in a chair, or on the ground.
- Keep your back straight.
- Let your shoulders drop.
- Close your eyes.

Step Two
- Be with your breath.
- Bring your attention to the movement of your breath in your body.
- There's no need to change anything at this point, just experience it and become aware of it.

Step Three
- Focus on breathing in through your nose.
- Notice the air filling your lungs.
- Hold it there for a few seconds.

Step Four
- Breathe out through your mouth or nose.

Step Five
- You will have thoughts.
- Don't worry about them and don't try to stop these thoughts.
- Just let them be, without attaching any meaning to them.
- Let them leave, not having any effect on you.

How did this feel to you?
_____
_____
_____

How did you feel different when doing this?
_____
_____
_____

Describe how you felt in control, or not.
_____
_____
_____

Describe if you worried about anything or how you felt calm.
_____
_____

What is Abdominal Breathing?

By feeling the physical sensation of your breath you can bring awareness to both your body and your breathing.

To begin, place your hand on your abdomen and feel your ab muscles rise and fall with your breath. How does this feel?

_____
_____
_____

Next, bring your complete mindful consciousness to the sensation of your belly rising and falling in unison with your breath. How does this affect your awareness?

_____
_____
_____

Now, allow your breath to slow down and become calm as you make the connection between your thoughts, emotions, and physical experience. How did this work for you?

_____
_____
_____

If anxious thoughts arise, acknowledge them and bring your awareness back to your breath.
Did anxious thought arise? If so, describe them and how you were able to focus on your breath.

_____
_____
_____

Did you find yourself judging any aspects of your experience? Explain.

_____
_____
_____

If you found yourself judging any aspects of your experience, imagine yourself breathing out the judgment with each breath as you let go and surrender to the present moment. Was that helpful?

_____
_____
_____

If any of these abdominal breathing practices didn't work for you, keep trying. Don't give up!

Have You Tried Breathing to Avoid Being Judgmental?

You may be asking yourself "How can I possibly turn off the automatic-judgment machine that lives in my head?" This process takes time and practice but it can be done! Implement it the next time that you find yourself judging yourself, other people, or situations that are related to one of your everyday hassles.

One of my ongoing daily hassles and how it causes me worry, anxiety, and/or stress: _____
_____
_____
_____
_____

Relax and focus on your breathing.
Count ten breaths as you follow your breath coming into your body and leaving your body.

How does this feel? _____
_____
_____

Step back and observe.
Notice that the part of you investigating this judgment is not itself judging anything; it's simply observing bodily sensations, thoughts, and emotions with balance and curiosity.

What do you observe in this situation? _____
_____
_____

Suspend judgments.
Rather than allowing your thoughts and emotions to take over, simply observe and accept the situation for what it is.

How can you observe and accept the hassle for what it is – just a hassle? _____
_____
_____

Respond rationally.
Respond from a mindful state rather than a reactive state.

How can you respond mindfully? _____
_____
_____

How Can You Practice Mindful Appreciation?

Being mindful also includes remembering to be appreciative of the people in your life, accepting them for who they are as human beings, and exploring why you appreciate each of them.

Identify people in your life whom you appreciate and write about why you appreciate them.

People in My Life	Why I Appreciate This Person

Take the time to be mindful and on the next page write a note of appreciation to one of the people you wrote about above.

I Appreciate You!

Can You Maintain Your Focus?

Mindfulness can be developed through simply observing and attending to an object. By directing your attention outwardly from yourself to an object can lead to present moment, non-judgmental mindfulness.

Try the following activity for two or three minutes and then journal about how the activity affected you.

- Sit with your posture straight.
- Choose an object on which you would like to concentrate.
- Relax and focus your attention on the object for as long as you can.
- Try not to let your gaze wander, and if it does, return your focus.
- Do not judge or think about the object in any way, simply observe it.
- Appreciate the qualities of the object.

Describe how this experience felt.

___

How hard was it to maintain your focus? Why?

___

What thoughts popped into your head?

___

In what ways did you try to escape the observation of your object?

___

How Can You Be More Aware of Your Body?

It is important to bring awareness to your body. By doing this, you can bring attention to the connection between your thoughts and emotions and your body sensations. This activity will allow you to become more aware of the ways that worry, anxiety, and/or stress can manifest itself in your body. You can easily become more aware of the various sensations throughout your body in a non-judgmental manner.

Read through these instructions first and then practice the activity.

Settle into your body either lying down or sitting in a chair. Feel the weight of your body on the floor or against the chair. Breathe normally and slowly. Be with and accept whatever sensations you notice.

Now begin scanning your body by spending a few seconds noticing the various bodily sensations.

Start with your left leg. Observe and become aware of your toes, foot, calf, shin, knee, thigh, and your whole leg. Then do the same with your right leg. What do you notice?

_____

_____

Observe and become aware of your hips and buttocks. What do you notice?

_____

_____

Now observe and become aware of your lower back, the middle of your back and your upper back and shoulders. What do you notice?

_____

_____

Observe both arms in the same manner: your fingers, hands, elbows, etc. What do you notice?

_____

_____

Lastly, observe and become aware of your head, ears, jaws, nose, and face. What do you notice?

_____

_____

How did you feel after doing this exercise?

_____

_____

Are You Thinking Again?

We are often thinking things without our even being aware that we are doing so. This can be a problem for many people. Thoughts and judgments are generated automatically and can interfere with one's awareness and concentration, keeping one from being in the present. This allows one to worry, be anxious, and/or feel stressed about everyday hassles.

To mindfully overcome this, you can learn to bring attention to these thoughts by labelling them. Try the following activity and then write about the experience.

Sit comfortably and feel your feet grounded on the floor.

Bring awareness to your breathing by observing each breath coming into your body through your nose, and then feeling each breath leave through your mouth. Do this for about five minutes, simply concentrating on your breathing.

From time to time, you will notice your attention being taken away from your breath by intruding thoughts. Each time this happens, you can silently say to yourself "I'm thinking…" and then return to your breathing.

Do this without becoming agitated, judging yourself negatively, or criticizing yourself. Each time it happens, silently remind yourself "I'm thinking again."

Each time your mind wanders from your breathing, don't judge the thoughts as good or bad. Label them as "thinking" and return to the observation of your breathing.

What are your thoughts about this experience?

_____
_____
_____
_____
_____
_____
_____
_____
_____
_____
_____
_____

Can You Be Thankful?

It is important to be introspective as you develop a state of mindfulness. It can be challenging to incorporate new healthy habits, but you can do it! We often forget to be thankful for the everyday wonderments in our life.

Follow the instructions below, and then respond to each of the sentence starters by identifying what you are thankful for in this present moment.

1) Set time aside to simply sit quietly.
2) Find a way that you will not be distracted by outside people and things.
3) Turn off all of your technological devices.
4) Sit for a few minutes and try to block thoughts that intrude.
5) Respond to the following sentence starters.

I am thankful for...

I am thankful for...

I am thankful for...

I am thankful for...

I am thankful for...

And most of all, I am thankful for...

Whole Person Associates is the leading publisher of training resources for professionals who empower people to create and maintain healthy lifestyles. Our creative resources will help you work effectively with your clients in the areas of stress management, wellness promotion, mental health, and life skills.

Please visit us at our web site: **WholePerson.com**. You can check out our entire line of products, place an order, request our print catalog, and sign up for our monthly special notifications.

Whole Person Associates
800-247-6789
Books@WholePerson.com